College Life

Campus Voices

Written by College Students · Compiled by Paul Buchanan & Paula Miller

Regal

From Gospel Light
Ventura, California, U.S.A.

Published by Regal
From Gospel Light
Ventura, California, U.S.A.
www.regalbooks.com
Printed in the U.S.A.

Library of Congress Cataloging-in-Publication Data
Campus voices : a student-to student guide to college life / compiled and edited by Paula Miller and Paul Buchanan.
    p. cm.
 ISBN 978-0-8307-4788-7 (trade paper)
1. College students—Religious life. 2. Universities and colleges—Religion. I. Miller, Paula. II. Buchanan, Paul, 1959-
 BV4531.3.C3655 2009
 248.8'34—dc22
 2008047993

3 4 5 6 7 8 9 10 / 15 14 13 12 11 10

Rights for publishing this book outside the U.S.A. or in non-English languages are administered by Gospel Light Worldwide, an international not-for-profit ministry. For additional information, please visit www.glww.org, email info@glww.org, or write to Gospel Light Worldwide, 1957 Eastman Avenue, Ventura, CA 93003, U.S.A.

Contents

Part 3: Voices of Forgiveness and Encouragement

Part 4: Voices of Identity and Personality

Part 5: Voices of Love and Friendship

Part 6: Voices of Suffering and Hope

Part 7: Voices of Humanity and the World

Part 8: Voices of Growth and Decision

A Note from the Compilers

Everyone wants to have a voice. In your collegiate world, individuals regularly offer their opinions in class discussion, on T-shirts, in text messages, campus blogs and Facebook walls. In this devotional, Christian college students from various schools across the country share their essays about university life. Their stories are honest, insightful and relevant. No matter where you are in your academic career, you are bound to confront faith-testing predicaments along with flashes of enlightenment. Facing those times will give you much to think about, and maybe even a lot to say.

We hope that *Campus Voices: A Student to Student Guide to College Life* offers you the encouragement you need to face the demands of higher education. This book gives you a chance to express yourself as well. Its journal pages offer space to explore your thoughts on the struggles you face, the temptations that weigh upon you, the victories you win and the questions you ponder.

Read, write and pray, knowing that you are not alone. Your fellow students have faced an array of challenges and survived. With God's help, you will too.

May God bless,
Paula Miller
Paul Buchanan

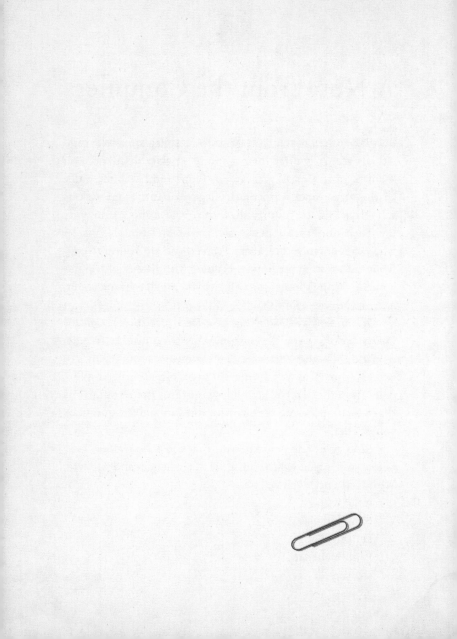

Part 1

Voices of Experience and Insight

Get wisdom, get understanding: forget it not; neither decline from the words of my mouth. Forsake her not, and she shall preserve thee: love her, and she shall keep thee. Wisdom is the principal thing; therefore get wisdom: and with all thy getting get understanding.

PROVERBS 4:5-7, KJV

They are never alone that are accompanied with noble thoughts.

SIR PHILIP SIDNEY

Amazing Times

By Jennifer Tibbett, Azusa Pacific University

But they that wait upon the LORD shall renew their strength;
they shall mount up with wings as eagles; they shall run, and not be
weary; and, they shall walk, and not faint.

ISAIAH 40:31, *KJV*

I sit here as a senior in college, on the brink of what feels like the rest of my life, and I wonder what life would have been like had I not spent the past four years in school. I remember showing up to my dorm freshman year, belongings and angst-ridden parents in tow, peering around at a campus filled with cool kids. I wouldn't fit in; I just knew it. It was going to be high school all over again. As I lugged my comforter up the fourth flight of stairs, with a chirping RA (who was toting my clothes) bringing up the rear, I cringed with sheer terror. *Welcome to the next four years of your life!* I thought.

And I'll admit the past four years have been staggeringly difficult. Never in my life have I lived off so little food and sleep and survived on so much ramen and coffee. Adjusting to having a roommate was, at times, worse than Chinese water torture. I rarely had enough money and too often ended up relying on Emergen-C to keep me functioning through an awful bout of the flu. I pulled numerous horrid all-nighters, failed several midterms and lost count of how many times I ditched class to catch a nap. Many times, my faith in God was the only thing that kept me afloat.

However, I also had the most amazing times of my life. College will be the best years of your life, too. You will listen to lectures that will permanently alter your pattern of thought. You will enroll in classes that you are overjoyed to attend. You will make friends that you will love and remember—maybe until the day you die. There will be late-night runs to In-N-Out Burger followed by trips to the local donut shop. There will be spur-of-the-moment beach trips and club hopping. You will tell your children about these memories one day and laugh. And, unlike high school, you may even mourn your graduation.

Isaiah 40:31 perfectly describes the wonder of college for me. Perhaps your experience will be the same. There will be hard work galore, and you'll find seemingly insurmountable obstacles in your path. You'll wonder who you're supposed to be, what you're supposed to do and where you're supposed to go—and it's possible that none of these questions will be answered. College takes patience, a sense of humor and reliance on God. He has a plan for you, believe it or not.

You'll start off walking, then running and eventually flying. Although you'll get tired and sick and lonely, look to the Lord and find joy in your trials. They pay off in the end.

Journal Response

Jesus Christ is the same yesterday and today and forever.
HEBREWS 13:8

Because of the Lord's great love we are not consumed, for his compassions
never fail. They are new every morning; great is your faithfulness.
I say to myself, "The Lord is my portion; therefore I will wait for him."
LAMENTATIONS 3:22-24

The beginning of a new school year can seem daunting. Perhaps you feel overwhelmed by academic expectations, personal challenges or financial obligations. Yet God is unchanging and ever-present to guide and comfort you. Consider ways in which God's faithfulness can encourage you in a time of uncertainty.

A Day in Life

By Rebecca Whitten Poe, Union University

Now listen, you who say, "Today or tomorrow we will go to this or that city, spend a year there, carry on business and make money." Why, you do not even know what will happen tomorrow. What is your life? You are a mist that appears for a little while and then vanishes. Instead, you ought to say, "If it is the Lord's will, we will live and do this or that."

JAMES 4:13-15

February 5, 2008, was a pretty normal Tuesday. I went to class, complained about cafeteria food and put off doing homework. When the tornado sirens in the residence complexes went off, we all went to the downstairs rooms as usual, grumbling about having to leave our TV programs and half-written papers.

At 7:03 P.M., my life as a college student changed forever. Suddenly, I was on the floor, pulling the screaming freshmen girls under me and covering their heads with my hands as the room shook and debris fell. My ears popped. I looked up to see the ceiling tiles jumping. *Well, Lord,* I thought, *here I go.*

That night was one of the most surreal experiences of my life. In a matter of seconds, my quiet campus was transformed into what looked like a war zone. Panicked voices called out to each other in the dark, and flashlight-illuminated figures crouched over writhing bodies. The next morning, I looked in awe at the wreckage that had been my dorm building.

Disaster relief professionals said that the F4 tornado should have claimed at least a hundred lives at Union University. But miraculously, even though dozens of students were buried in the rubble, not a single student died, and only two sustained serious injuries.

As Christians, we always talk about being ready to die, but how many of us actually think about the fact that we are not guaranteed tomorrow? It's amazing how much I learned as my world caved in around me—literally. For the first time, I realized just how great God is. I realized that I shouldn't let myself be consumed by this life, worrying about what to major in or what grad school to apply to or if I'll get married.

On February 5, I faced my own death. And that was okay. On February 6, I woke up and faced my life—and knew that I wouldn't be living it for myself anymore. Ultimately, what matters in this life is how you live for the next one.

Tornado Facts and Safety Tips

It's possible for tornadoes to develop in any state, but most occur in states across the Plains, Midwest and Southeast. Tornadoes develop from severe thunderstorm systems that arise in the early spring and summer months. Tornadoes can move in any direction but generally move from southwest to northeast at an average speed of 30 mph. When the National Weather Service issues a tornado *watch*, it means that the conditions are right for the formation of tornadoes. However, a *warning* means that tornadoes have actually been sighted or detected by radar.

When a tornado warning sounds, you should take shelter immediately and remember the following:

- If you're inside a structure, go to the lowest level.

- If a basement is not available, seek shelter in the most interior room (closet or bathroom), putting as many walls as possible between you and the tornado.

- Hide under a piece of heavy furniture, like a table or desk, and use your arms to protect your head and neck. Or use a mattress and cover with a blanket.

- If you're in a mobile home, exit immediately and seek shelter in a sturdy building, if one is nearby.

- If you're in a vehicle and have time, take shelter in a sound building. On open roads, drive perpendicular to the tornado's movement to avoid or outrun the funnel cloud.

- If you're outside with no shelter in sight, as a last resort, lie down flat in the lowest spot, like a ditch or depression. Watch out for flying debris, and cover your head.

Warnings About Tornado Safety

- Don't open windows before seeking shelter.

- Don't take shelter under a bridge or freeway overpass. Strong winds tunneling through such narrow passages can sweep you away.

- Don't try to outrun a tornado in a car when you're in urban regions or in areas of congested traffic.

The Fujita-Pearson Scale

Tornadoes are classified by the following scale:

F-5 Destroys homes; blows vehicles long distances. Extensive destruction (261-318 mph winds).

F-4 Destroys outer walls on solid structures; moves large vehicles; levels homes (207-260 mph winds).

F-3 Damages roofs and exterior walls; overturns large trucks or trains; uproots trees (158-205 mph winds).

F-2 Downs trees; destroys lightweight structures; lifts off roofs (113-157 mph winds).

F-1 Threatens damage to mobile homes, roofs, vehicles and other lightweight structures (73-112 mph winds).

F-0 Breaks tree branches; dislodges brick chimneys. Slight wind damage (40-72 mph winds).[1]

Note

1. "Are You Ready?" FEMA, May 30, 2008. http://www.fema.gov/areyouready/ tornadoes.shtm; "Tornado Safety . . . What You Need to Know NOW!" NOAA: National Severe Storms Laboratory, April 2, 2007. http://www.nssl. noaa.gov/ edu/safety/tornado.html; "Fujita-Pearson Scale of Tornado Intensity," Disaster Center. http://www.disastercenter.com/tornado/fujipear.htm.

Choice Matters

By Christopher Louis Frank, Miami University

Today I have given you the choice between life and death, between blessings and curses. I call on heaven and earth to witness the choice you make. Oh, that you would choose life, so that you and your descendents might live! You can make this choice by loving the LORD your God, obeying him, and committing yourself firmly to him.
DEUTERONOMY 30:19-20, *NLT*

One of the greatest lessons I've learned from college is that choice matters. It's the message Moses spoke of in Deuteronomy 30. The importance of choices is something I instinctively know, yet seldom evaluate. What I must consider is this: the choices I make today, be they good or bad, affect tomorrow.

Think about it: Choose not to brush your teeth today, get gingivitis tomorrow. Choose to take your vitamins today, be healthier tomorrow. Choose to study today, do well on the test tomorrow. Choose to waste today, be behind tomorrow. No matter what we choose today, consequences will be realized tomorrow. Maybe not tomorrow as in the next day, but tomorrow as in next week, next month or 40 years from now.

In Deuteronomy, Moses had just seen the Lord bring Israel through the wilderness and into the Promised Land. As God would have it, this would be Moses' final address to the nation before God called him home, for not even Moses would enter this land. In Moses' speech, I think that he is telling us that we have choices to make every day—choices between loving and obeying God and committing ourselves to Him or taking our own path.

So here's the big thing to consider: Today, we can choose whatever we want. We can ask God to give us discernment and wisdom to make the right choice. Maybe it's a choice not to go to a party or to join in a certain negative conversation. Maybe it's a choice to have a quiet time instead of sleeping in. Maybe it's helping that person we sit next to in history class.

The choice is ours. Let's choose wisely.

Journal Response

Now fear the Lord and serve him with all faithfulness. Throw away the gods your forefathers worshiped beyond the River and in Egypt, and serve the Lord. But if serving the Lord seems undesirable to you, then choose for yourselves this day whom you will serve, whether the gods your forefathers served beyond the River, or the gods of the Amorites, in whose land you are living. But as for me and my household, we will serve the Lord.

JOSHUA 24:14-15

In this passage, Joshua is challenging the Israelites to serve God as they take possession of the Promised Land. He's asking them to choose a path for their future. Is decision making hard for you? If so, why? What difficult decisions are you facing this year? How can you involve God in your choices?

_____

_____

_____

_____

_____

Loving the Sisterhood

By Alexandra Kerr, Azusa Pacific University

*Show proper respect to everyone: Love the brotherhood
of believers, fear God, honor the king.*

1 PETER 2:17

One of the most frightening moments in my life was the day I became an only child with 32 siblings. Though I had no brothers or sisters growing up, my arrival at Azusa Pacific University would finally allow me the opportunity to feel that special sibling bond. I spent my first day at college getting to know my 32 new sisters, the ladies of Trinity Hall, fifth floor, north side.

Moving in with nearly 10 times the number of people I was accustomed to was only the first of many shocks. I was quickly forced to acclimate to a completely foreign concept: the roommate. I would soon find that personal space and alone time were a privilege offered only to upperclassmen in apartments, leaving us dorm-bound freshmen to a life of nonstop girl talk, shower parties and late-night roommate chats.

Although I hadn't expected the university to provide me with a personal restroom, adjusting to 12 showers and 8 toilets with a constant stream of 32 primping girls took some getting used to. In a poor attempt at maintaining some degree of privacy, I often waited until the wee hours to go in the communal restroom. I became accustomed to taking 2:00 A.M. showers.

What were once solitary rituals, like brushing my teeth or straightening my hair, quickly became the most social part of my day. I felt I had to prep myself to go into the bathroom, rather than the other way around. On the plus side, there was a never-ending supply of sounding boards for how my hair and makeup looked each morning. Before long, over the tiny sinks and lukewarm showers, we swapped everything from shampoo and lotion to romantic advice and study tips.

Conflicts inevitably arose, whether over a missing jacket, borrowed shoes or a hairdryer gone MIA. I soon learned an art form once solely reserved for siblings, and I finally understood why God used the metaphor of brothers and sisters when He told us how to treat one another. In a matter of moments, hot tempers would cool and forbearance and mutual understanding would replace the most heated exchanges. Despite our frustrations, we were hall-mates. We were sisters.

Through my dorm experience, God taught me to love the sisterhood of believers.

Ten Tips for Surviving Dorm Life

1. Explore Your Options

Know what dormitory options exist on your campus so that you can request the best fit. Ask other residents for advice and ideas in finding a dorm and setting up your room.

2. Contact Your Roommate Early

Getting in touch with roommates before the semester starts helps with coordinating things like room furniture. Getting to know new roommates before you move in can eliminate surprises.

3. Set Boundaries Early

Inform your roommate early on about what is satisfactory or off-limits for you. You might think sharing socks is perfectly acceptable, while your roommate may be horrified by the idea!

4. Be Considerate

Being respectful of your roommate and dormmates will stop most problems before they begin. Put their needs above your own, and you'll find that getting along will be much easier.

5. Be Vocal

If you feel your boundaries are being crossed, let your roommate know. Don't drag conflicts out. Nothing is worse than thick tension in a small living space.

6. Leave Your Door Open

Keeping your door open when you are in your room lets people know you are available. Everyone else is feeling as shy and awkward as you are; open doors are much more inviting than closed ones.

7. Be Informed

Regularly check the information boards. Keeping up to date on campus happenings is vital. You don't want to find that you missed out on free chocolate bunnies simply because you missed the signs.

8. Get Involved

Dorms often have student-led organizations. Join dorm-floor boards, go to floor meetings, and attend student government dorm committee meetings. Ask where you can help out! Influence your community!

9. Get to Know Your Representation

Resident assistants, senators or student representatives act on your behalf. Getting to know them personally can have its advantages. Who knows? They may have organized the giving away of chocolate bunnies!

10. Learn to Adapt

This is the most important rule. Dorm life is a unique living situation. You can have some control if you are willing to adapt. Expand your comfort zone and learn to let things go. Choose your battles wisely, and be willing to have fun!

—Emily Brown, Biola University

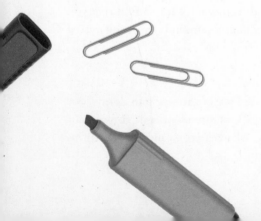

Building Hope

By Nathan Barstad, Biola University

Not that I am speaking of being in need, for I have learned in whatever situation I am to be content. I know how to be brought low, and I know how to abound. In any and every circumstance, I have learned the secret of facing plenty and hunger, abundance and need. I can do all things through him who strengthens me.

PHILIPPIANS 4:11-13, *ESV*

When I started college, I wish I would have understood this truth: Everything is going to be okay because God is in control, even if I'm not. During my first two years of school, I was scared that I wouldn't have enough money or that I would incur too much loan debt, so I became angry at everyone. First, I was angry with God for not making me rich like I thought everyone else was. Second, I was angry with everyone else for being rich. Third, I was angry with myself for not knowing what to do since I wasn't rich.

I was a lot like the disciples, who found themselves out at sea in the midst of a life-threatening storm with Jesus, asleep in the boat (see Mark 4:35-41). They were scared out of their minds that they were going to drown. After they woke Jesus up, He asked them, "Why are you so afraid? Have you still no faith?" From all appearances, they did have faith, since they turned to Jesus. Yet, like me, they were still scared.

My attitude changed when the Lord brought Philippians 4:11-13 to my attention through my church small-group leader. As I thought about these verses, I realized that my circumstances are not the gauge by which I measure my life or how it is going; I ought to measure my life by how much God loves me. Because He loves me more than I'll ever know, and because He has given me all things in Christ, my life is going very, very well.

I can rejoice now (even though I still don't have tons of money, and I've got lots of loans to pay off) because my contentment isn't determined by something like wealth or poverty. It is determined by God's greatness shown to me in His grace through Jesus.

So, I can be in a storm like the disciples were and not freak out. Not because I'm so cool or spiritual, or because I've learned to annihilate my emotions like an ascetic Buddhist, but because my confidence is in Jesus. If He wants me to go through a storm or allows my boat to capsize, I will trust Him, because He is sovereign and He is good.

My hope is built on nothing less
than Jesus' blood and righteousness.
EDWARD MOTE

Journal Response

Therefore I tell you, do not worry about your life, what you will eat or drink, or about your body, what you will wear. Is not life more important than food, and the body more important than clothes?

MATTHEW 6:25

Which of you, if his son asks for bread, will give him a stone? Or if he asks for a fish, will give him a snake? If you, then, though you are evil, know how to give good gifts to your children, how much more will your Father in heaven give good gifts to those who ask him!

MATTHEW 7:9-11

What dilemmas are you facing this semester? Is it hard for you to trust God to help you? Why or why not? Consider making a list of those situations that cause you worry and offering them to God in prayer.

_____

_____

_____

_____

_____

_____

_____

_____

_____

_____

_____

Major Choices

By Andrew Lawson Crist, Abilene Christian University

*Look at the birds of the air; they do not sow or reap or
store away in barns, and yet your heavenly Father feeds them.
Are you not much more valuable than they?*
MATTHEW 6:26

There was one aspect of college I didn't see coming: the classes
I took in college were not all chosen *for* me as they were in high
school. I had to choose my own classes and, thus, my career.

I started my freshman year at Abilene Christian University
as a business major. Whenever I met a new person that first
week—which was every five minutes—I would answer the three
basic questions common to all freshmen:

> "What's your name?" (Andrew Crist.)

> "Where are you from?" (Saint Louis, Missouri.)

> "Cool, what's your major?" (Business.)

It seemed so easy, but then school started. I attended only
two business classes before going to my advisor and changing
my major to biology.

When I went to my first biology classes, I immediately felt
relief in my wise decision. I couldn't figure out why I had wanted
to be a business major, considering my love for biology and my

desire to be a doctor, which I'd considered during my last two years of high school.

I now knew what I wanted to do. My future was clear.

That was until I studied a semester abroad in Oxford and had the opportunity to experience a whole new culture in a whole new country. When I returned to West Texas, my dreams of becoming a doctor faded.

During my senior year, with umpteen credit hours behind me, I made another visit to my advisor and changed my major again, this time to English. It seemed like a good fit for me. I loved literature. But I also knew that I didn't want to teach—and what else is there to do with an English degree?

I felt like my future was being tossed around like the crimson windsock that hung from my neighbor's porch. Watching the windsock, my worry grew, but I was calmed when I shifted my attention to the warblers perched in the tree *behind* the windsock and remembered God's provision for all birds.

Since God provides for all birds, I now feel comfort in knowing that He provides for all majors, too, be they business, biology, English—or even political science.

How to Choose a Major

Consider your interests. Perhaps your hobbies or your favorite leisure activities can lead you to a field of study.

Assess your academic strengths. What subject in high school did you enjoy or excel in? What do you like to read?

Reflect on your talents. Being musical or athletic, for example, may influence your choices for a vocation.

Visit your campus career-counseling center to obtain information about study options.

Take a skills or aptitude assessment test to help define your strengths.

Talk to professors and professionals in various fields to learn about what is required to perform various jobs or to enter specific occupations.

Research which employment fields will be expanding or in need of personnel in the next 10 years. Decide if any of those markets are of interest to you.

Seek internships in a field you find interesting. Internships provide hands-on experience that let you know whether you can succeed in a specific work environment.

Select a major based on your own desires and motivations. Do not feel pressure to become a business major simply because others have expectations that you should become a business-person some day.

Do not be afraid to change majors if you decide that your first (or second) choice is not well suited to your interests, talents and abilities.

Blessed

By Jennifer K. Rickabaugh, Biola University

*I will make you into a great nation. I will bless you and
make you famous, and you will be a blessing to others. I will bless
those who bless you and curse those who treat you with contempt.
All the families on the earth will be blessed through you.*

GENESIS 12:2-3, *NLT*

I love to listen to music while studying. Every once in a while,
I borrow a roommate's music or download a new album off
iTunes to motivate me to study. There are two songs I have been
constantly putting on my study mix during my senior year:
"The Blessing" by John Waller and "Blessed" by Martina McBride.

I have fallen in love with these songs because they express
what I feel in ways I cannot always articulate. "The Blessing" is
essentially about the Body of Christ and how we are called to be
blessings to the world. This song humbles me. I chose to come
to a Christian university so that I could be challenged in my
faith, so that I could take Bible classes, and so that other believers in Christ could encourage me. I hope that in these college
years I have been a "blessing for life." I want to be known "by the
fruit I leave behind." I know that my college and my fellow classmates are my blessings.

I can sum up my college experience by saying it was a blessing from God. The words of the chorus of "Blessed" by Martina

McBride describe it well: "I have been blessed with so much more than I deserve." Like McBride's song says, I, too, thank God for all He's given to me.

I pray that God blesses you with your college experience. I hope that you find your way and that you walk proudly with Christ. Rely on Him, and He will "be a blessing for life." Be encouraged by other believers and bless the people you encounter in life.

Journal Response

Blessed is the man who does not walk in the counsel of the wicked or stand in the way of sinners or sit in the seat of mockers. But his delight is in the law of the Lord, and on his law he meditates day and night.

PSALM 1:1-2

Consider the ways that God has blessed you. How has your faith been strengthened by God's blessings? In what ways could you "pay it forward" by helping or encouraging someone else?

_____

_____

_____

_____

_____

_____

_____

_____

_____

_____

8

Don't Worry About a Thing

By Pierre Collins, Liberty University

Do not be anxious about anything, but in everything,
by prayer and petition, with thanksgiving, present your requests to God.
And the peace of God, which transcends all understanding,
will guard your hearts and your minds in Christ Jesus.

PHILIPPIANS 4:6-7

Finances have been a struggle for me. I didn't know if I was going to be coming back to school the second semester of my freshman year because I didn't have the money. My mom sent me back to school anyway. All that first week I complained like a little kid, because I thought I would be kicked out of my dorm room and have to drop out. I even called my mom a few times and told her to come pick me up, but she told me I needed to have faith. I still hadn't done financial check-in by the first day of classes, but things worked out, and I was able to get a loan to cover the costs.

My second year, I faced the same situation, and that made me very angry. I just wanted to move away somewhere and start doing something else. It seemed even more impossible for me to get into school, because this time I didn't even have a room. I was able to get a special scholarship to get me into school, but rather than being in the dorm room I had picked, I was placed somewhere else. I ended up having a better year than I would have had in the dorm I had originally chosen. God does everything for a reason, and His plans are better than ours.

When I came back the second semester of my third year, my attitude was completely different from that of the previous two years. I knew that God would provide the money; and I knew that if He didn't, He had other plans. Once again, He provided for me.

As I look to the future, I know that there will be more struggles ahead but that God will guide me through them. God wants us to take our concerns to Him and trust in Him fully.

College Students and College Loans: How Much Is Too Much?

The National Center for Education Statistics reports that more than 60 percent of college students rely on loans to pay for their education. There are many options for getting student aid, and each campus has a financial aid department to help students locate sources to meet the costs of getting a degree. If you can't attend college without borrowing funds, keep these tips in mind:

- Exhaust all grant and scholarship opportunities before considering a college loan.

- Don't borrow more than you need, even if you qualify for a higher amount.

- Find work during summers and get a job on campus to offset the amount you have to borrow.

- Be aware that federal loans carry a service charge of 3 to 4 percent. So the amount paid to your college account may be slightly less than the amount awarded you.

- Consider that your total loan debt at graduation should not be more than your first year's salary once you start working after college.

There are many ways to count the cost of borrowing to finance your education. With the help of an online student loan calculator, you can determine the price tag for federal student loans.

Imagine that you qualified for both a Federal Perkins Loan and a Federal Stafford Student Loan. If you borrowed the allowed amount of $4,000 for a Perkins Loan each year for four years, at graduation, you would owe $16,000. In addition, if you took out a Stafford Loan, borrowing slightly less than the maximum available, you might accumulate an additional $17,125. Here's where the calculations are helpful. After graduation, your total debt with principal and interest would be $42,463. You would have 10 years to repay the loan, with rates varying from 5 to 6.8 percent interest. So your combined monthly payments would be around $354. If you earn a salary of $40,000 during your first year after college, then those loan payments would amount to a bit more than 10 percent of your annual income.

Loan programs provide students with the opportunity to fund an education. They can be great resources. Just be responsible and informed as you seek ways to finance your schooling, and count the cost of those loans before you graduate.[1]

Note

1. *The Project on Student Debt.* http://projectonstudentdebt.org; "Student Loan Calculator," collegeboard.com, Inc. http://apps.collegeboard.com/fincalc/sla.jsp; Mary Hunt, "Don't Get Over Your Head in College Debt," *Everyday Cheapskate*, June 3, 2008.

Part 2

Voices of Faith
and Doubt

*Now faith is being sure of what we hope for and certain of what we
do not see. This is what the ancients were commended for.
By faith we understand that the universe was formed at God's command,
so that what is seen was not made out of what was visible.*

HEBREWS 11:1-3

*I know there is a Supreme Being who rules the affairs of men and
whose goodness and mercy have always followed the American people,
and I know He will not turn from us now if we humbly and
reverently seek His powerful aid.*

GROVER CLEVELAND

9

The Mountaintop

By Lauri Schakett, University of California at Santa Barbara

Be still, and know that I am God!
PSALM 46:10, *NLT*

Last summer, I was in one of the most breathtaking and peaceful places on this earth, and never before had I felt more desperate, confused and hopeless. A week had already passed on my journey to the Promised Land, and my eyes, heart and mind had already taken in so much information I thought I could not possibly store one more thing in my brain. I was loving the trip; I had walked where Jesus walked, sat where He sat and swam where He . . . walked. I had been looking forward to the hike up to the lookout over the Sea of Galilee, where scholars have concluded that Jesus ventured off on occasion to be in solitude and pray.

However, once I was on top of the mountain, blown about by the rushing wind that raced around my legs and through my hair, I felt my heart tangle as my brothers and sisters sang hymns to the Creator of it all. My eyes had been opened to the reality of the Scriptures, but I was squinting to see how I would be able to bring everything I had learned home with me.

The irony was astounding: I was in one of the most serene places on the planet, yet I was fretting over my life back home—oceans away. I couldn't forget the schoolwork, relationships, responsibilities and obligations that awaited me. How could I go back to my routine with everything that I had learned? At the same time, I had no idea how to change my life completely. Overwhelmed by the vastness of God and the constriction of myself, I could not grasp how I could ever do even a fraction of what He would want me to do. I was destined to fail. I had no hope.

Suddenly I felt a whisper in the forceful breeze: *Be still, and know that I am God.*

As I walked slowly down from my mountaintop experience, I was free to obey that command. I am to cease striving (another translation of "be still," *NASB*) and know that He is God. As I rest in the knowledge of His deity, I gain freedom to run with endurance the race that He has set before me (see Hebrews 12:1), because in Him I cannot fail. I thank God that "I can do everything *through him* who gives me strength" (Philippians 4:13, emphasis added).

How to Find Peace in the World

There's actually a think tank devoted to finding the most peaceful place in the world. The Institute for Economics and Peace, in cooperation with a group from the University of Sydney, has developed a Global Peace Index, which measures the peacefulness of 140 countries using a 1-5 scale, with 1 being the most peaceful/least stressful and 5 being the least peaceful/most violent or stressful. Here are a few rankings from the 2008 study:

Iceland: Ranked the most peaceful country
Rate of violent crime: 1
Rate of distrust in other citizens: 1
Percentage of those who pursue higher education: 67.7
Life expectancy: 81.1 years

Japan: Ranked 5
Rate of violent crime: 1
Rate of distrust in other citizens: 2
Percentage of those who pursue higher education: 54
Life expectancy: 82.1 years

Austria: Ranked 10
Rate of violent crime: 1
Rate of distrust in other citizens: 2
Percentage of those who pursue higher education: 49.8
Life expectancy: 79.4 years

Australia: Ranked 27
Rate of violent crime: 2
Rate of distrust in other citizens: 2
Percentage of those who pursue higher education: 54
Life expectancy: 80.6 years

United Kingdom: Ranked 49
Rate of violent crime: 1
Rate of distrust in other citizens: 3
Percentage of those who pursue higher education: 60.1
Life expectancy: 78.9 years

Cuba: Ranked 62
Rate of violent crime: 1
Rate of distrust in other citizens: 2
Percentage of those who pursue higher education: 53.6
Life expectancy: 77.3 years

China: Ranked 67

Rate of violent crime: 2

Rate of distrust in other citizens: 4

Percentage of those who pursue higher education: 19.1

Life expectancy: 71.8 years

United States: Ranked 97

Rate of violent crime: 1

Rate of distrust in other citizens: 2

Percentage of those who pursue higher education: 82.4

Life expectancy: 77.7 years

Russia: Ranked 131

Rate of violent crime: 3

Rate of distrust in other citizens: 4

Percentage of those who pursue higher education 68.2

Life expectancy: 65.5 years

Israel: Ranked 136

Rate of violent crime: 2

Rate of distrust in other citizens: 4

Percentage of those who pursue higher education: 56.5

Life expectancy: 79.7 years[1]

Note

1. "Global Peace Index Ratings," Vision of Humanity. http://www.visionofhumanity.org/gpi/results/rankings/2008/. All rankings by EIU analysts.

10

The Strength in Weakness

By Lisa Van Groningen, Trinity Christian College

Have I not commanded you? Be strong and courageous.
Do not be terrified; do not be discouraged, for the LORD
your God will be with you wherever you go.
JOSHUA 1:9

"God, grant me strength." How many times have we prayed these words? Strength to endure a bad roommate situation; strength to finish a paper; strength to help a friend through a tough time; strength to overcome the latest bout of homesickness; strength to make it through the last stretch before a break. The list goes on and on.

During my freshman and sophomore years, I prayed daily for strength. I prayed for strength during a difficult rooming situation; when my best friend decided to transfer back to her hometown, halfway across the country; when I could not find a summer job and had no clue how I would pay next year's tuition. But no matter how much I prayed for strength, I always felt something was missing. I kept praying, but it never felt like my strength came.

One day, I was reading a friend's Xanga, and I found what I was missing as I read a single sentence he wrote: *God, grant me the strength to be weak.* I had prayed to be strengthened—but this strength was based on something rotten, because I was praying for my own personal strength and not the strength found in

Christ. I realized I needed to be broken so that I could grow in the Lord's strength.

As much as we desire to be strong, we must make sure our strength is in the Lord and not in ourselves. We cannot be afraid to be weak. When we admit our weakness, we are capable of being broken; and only when we are broken can we truly grow in strength. Nothing can grow if it is not broken. God takes our brokenness and turns it into strength based on Him.

As a senior, my prayer is no longer, "God, grant me strength." Rather, it is now, "God, break me, so I can grow strong in You. Grant me the strength to be weak."

Journal Response

Praise be to the Lord, for he has heard my cry for mercy. The Lord is my strength and my shield; my heart trusts in him, and I am helped. My heart leaps for joy and I will give thanks to him in song. The Lord is the strength of his people, a fortress of salvation for his anointed one. Save your people and bless your inheritance; be their shepherd and carry them forever.

PSALM 28:6-9

Personal failures can often bring discouragement. In what areas of your life do you feel powerless to bring about change? How can relying on God's strength and mercy help you face disappointment?

_____

_____

_____

_____

_____

_____

To You I Call

By Kelline Linton, Abilene Christian University

To you I call, O LORD my Rock . . . Hear my cry for mercy as I call to you for help, as I lift up my hands to your Most Holy Place.

PSALM 28:1-2

I once read that David probably wrote Psalm 28 after his son had forced him from his own home. With these poignant words, David called for God's help, turning to a Most Holy Place. This was the Holy of Holies, the sacred area in the Tabernacle that housed the Ark of the Covenant.

The curious Israelites must have craved just a glimpse of that wonderful place where they could experience the Father's closeness. When Jesus died, the veil to the Holy of Holies was ripped apart. This event dramatically symbolized God welcoming all His children into a new intimacy with their Creator.

It is no wonder that when David was oppressed, he lifted his hands for God's mercy. It is no wonder that I lift my own hands to the Lord, crying for His peace. In such a way, I can relate to David's plea.

During my second year of college, I found myself desperate with the kind of despair I imagine gripped David as he hid in caves during cold desert nights. Within the space of one week, I failed two major exams, my boyfriend of six months dumped me, and my mom called to tell me that my four-year-old brother needed heart surgery. After that particular phone call, I remember sitting on the bathroom floor, my back against the door, sobbing until I felt nauseated. I needed to talk to someone—but to whom? My roommate and I were not on speaking terms. It was just me, locked in a grimy bathroom in a dusty, lonely city, an eight-hour drive from those I loved.

With a runny nose and streaming eyes, I lifted my hands for mercy. I needed help. Where was my Father?

When I called to God, I did not expect theatrics or sudden epiphanies. I just needed to know I was cherished and not alone.

And a soft peace came.

I had the sudden courage to call my mom back and the strength to talk to my little brother on the phone, joking about his day. I was able to experience what at other times I have to accept by faith: God is my life raft when the waves try to drown me.

We have a great high priest . . . Jesus the Son of God. . . .
We do not have a high priest who is unable to sympathize
with our weaknesses, but we have one who has been tempted
in every way, just as we are—yet was without sin. Let us then
approach the throne of grace with confidence . . .
and find grace to help us in our time of need.

HEBREWS 4:14-16

Dealing with Disasters

There's an adage that says, "Good things come one at a time, but bad things always come in threes." When those annoying, discouraging and, worse yet, tragic events arrive, what's a person to do? Here are some strategies for coping with life's dilemmas.

Pray for strength, peace and guidance. "You will keep him in perfect peace, whose mind is stayed on you, because he trusts in you" (Isaiah 26:3, *NKJV*).

Find trusted individuals to talk to. Expressing fears can often decrease anxious feelings.

Seek support. Search for a group of supportive, caring friends and family, other crisis survivors, or compassionate listeners who can encourage you.

Stay calm. Resist the panic impulse so that you can make sound decisions. "Now may the Lord of peace himself give you peace at all times and in every way" (2 Thessalonians 3:16).

Be flexible. Understand that solutions to a problem may be complex and time consuming. Expect the unexpected.

Remain hopeful. Believe that healing, solutions, recovery or just coping are possible. Pray for strength and trust.

Don't give up. Keep moving forward. Progress, no matter how small, offers hope.

Go to classes. Stick to routines.

Replace negative thoughts with positive ones. Read Scripture. Don't say, "Everything always goes wrong" or, "I can't survive this tragedy." Sing worship songs. Praise God. "We take captive every thought to make it obedient to Christ" (2 Corinthians 10:5).

Acknowledge the reality of the situation. Something bad has happened, but finding a way to cope will make you stronger. Seek help from professionals, such as psychologists, crisis counselors and pastors when necessary.

My Dumpster Runneth Over

By Dustin Everett Schamaun, Liberty University

I love the Lord, for he heard my voice; he heard my cry for mercy.
Because he turned his ear to me, I will call on him as long as I live.

PSALM 116:1-2

I came to college to see God. You might think, *What a weighty responsibility to put on one institution.* But I had expectations! I had given my life to Christ some five years earlier and dedicated my life to ministry in His service. You can imagine my unease, then, at the age of 18, feeling as if I had never truly *seen* God.

Some people see God in sunsets, birth, death, the coming of spring, world events and history. I remember driving through West Texas on vacation with my parents. I thought I saw God then, in the mountains, in the sweeping, sprawling vistas of green, orange and brown; but I never saw with certainty, only through the car window, and only at 70 miles per hour.

Some people see God in the everyday: in test grades or break-ups or a face going the other way in a crowd or a certain motion of the hands of a bag boy. I remember witnessing with missionaries in Belarus. I thought, perhaps, I saw God in the eyes of their congregation, but only for moments, like a fleeting glow or a reflection in some dim mirror.

My search for God in college began as soon as I stepped on campus. I looked into every eye and at every mountain. I listened intently to the speakers in chapel and to every note of every hymn sung in worship. More glimpses. Why could I never look God fully in His face?

It was not until months later I finally found Him. I was walking home from yet another worship service one night, past a row of dumpsters out behind the dorms, alone. It must have been something about the stench of the garbage—maybe it reminded me of the way I must have seemed to God before He ransomed me from my sin. On the other hand, perhaps it was the fact that, although I walked alone, I was in no way alone. I realized that God—the God I had spent so much time, effort and tears searching for—had been with me the entire time. He had never left me from the moment He entered my life some five years before. All I had to do to find Him was listen for His still, silent call.

Journal Response

Be content with what you have, because God has said, "Never will I leave you; never will I forsake you." So we say with confidence, "The Lord is my helper; I will not be afraid. What can man do to me?"

HEBREWS 13:5-6

Read Psalm 139:1-12, and then consider the ways God made Himself known to the David. What strength or comfort can you derive from David's song?

_____

_____

_____

_____

_____

_____

Don't Rock the Boat

By Rebecca Whitten Poe, Union University

The body is a unit, though it is made up of many parts;
and though all its parts are many, they form one body. So it is
with Christ. . . . If one part suffers, every part suffers with it;
if one part is honored, every part rejoices with it.
1 CORINTHIANS 12:12,26

I've never been the "sporty" girl. I was the one who got picked last for kickball and then spent the whole game trying to get out so she could sit down. But last year, I joined a rowing team at Oxford University, and over the course of the novice season I learned a lot—not only about rowing, but about my Christian walk as well.

Each crew team is made up of eight rowers who sit single file facing the back of the boat. They can't see where they're going, and they can't steer the boat even if they could see. The coxswain, who sits at the back of the boat, steering and shouting instructions and encouragement to the crew, is the only one who can see all the rowers and the river ahead. The rowers are absolutely dependent on his or her guidance.

Here's the thing about rowing: to move the boat through the water like it's supposed to, the rowers must work in perfect unison. Each stroke has to be exactly like the stroke of the person in front and the person behind. If you get off even a little, the boat will jerk and tip, making it more difficult for the other crew members to row.

In 1 Corinthians, Paul talks about how Christians make up the Body of Christ. All of us, you could say, are in one boat, and all of us are pulling together. Like a rowing crew, we have to make sure we're paying attention to the directions that our Divine Coxswain is giving us and that we're all living our lives in accordance with the way He tells us. And just as each rower's stroke affects the rest of the crew, the way we live our lives affects those around us.

We've all heard people talk about how hypocritical Christians are—drinking at the frat party on Saturday then leading worship on Sunday. People watch us, waiting to see if we'll live our lives the way that we, as Christians, say we will. When we start living out of sync with Christ, it makes every part of His body look bad.

So as we live our lives, we should remember to follow the calls of Christ . . . and not rock the boat!

The Sport of Rowing

Rowing is a popular Olympic and collegiate sport. Oxford and Cambridge held their first collegiate competition in 1829. Yale was the first United States university to offer rowing. The popularity of the sport quickly grew. In 1852, Yale and Harvard held their first rowing competition and have held their traditional regatta race every year since.

The early boats were made of wood, but modern ones are fashioned of lightweight composite materials like fiberglass. The eight-person shells are 60 feet long. Oarlocks hold the oars in place as the crew rows together in synchronized movement. Rowers face backwards, moving their individual oars to propel the boat forward. The action of rowing is a low-impact exercise that works all major muscle groups—the arms, legs and abdomen. The strongest rowers sit in the center of the craft.

The coxswain (pronounced *kok'san*) faces the rowers and must steer the boat. The coxswain motivates and coaches the crew. The coxswain's steady hand on the rudder and encouragement to the crew can mean the difference between winning or losing a race.[1]

Note

1. Information taken from www.southcrew.org; www.rowingnsw.asn.au; www.ashevillerowing.org; www.augustarowingclub.org; www.ashlandrowingclub.org.

A Whisper in the Wind

By Junghoo Song, Union University

The LORD said, "Go out and stand on the mountain in the presence of the LORD, for the LORD is about to pass by." Then a great and powerful wind tore the mountains apart and shattered the rocks before the LORD, but the LORD was not in the wind.

1 KINGS 19:11

I was the RA on duty that night. The television was on in the background, but I was merely pretending to listen:

If you are in the Jackson area, there are very strong indications of a tornado coming your way; take cover immediately.

I couldn't help but feel annoyed by the whole situation—the alarm, the phones, the TV announcers. Seconds later, Aaron Gilbert, another RA, and Matt Taylor, Aaron's roommate, came running into the commons yelling, "Get in the hallway! We need to take cover now—the tornado's here!"

We ran, but not into the hallway in the center of the commons; we ran to look out the door. Then we saw it—the black finger of God descending upon earth, destroying everything without even having to touch it. There we stood, frozen in awe and petrified in fear. A bolt of lightning streaked across the sky, screaming at us to run. Finally, someone yelled, "*RUN! GO, GO,*

GO!" We sprinted toward the hallway. The door we were stand-ing by was being tossed against the wind.

"That door's not going to shut!" Matt yelled as he ran to-ward the door. He struggled, but he never got it closed.

I stood there watching him wrestle against the wind, but before I could say the words, "Matt, forget the door and come back!" all the windows around me shattered. It was as if the glass evaporated into the air—it was wonderful and terrible all at once. A whirlwind came into the room and everything started swirling all around me. Time stood still while my mind captured images, sounds, smells and pain and seared them into my senses. Even now I can feel the cold, thin air that took my breath away as it sucked oxygen out of my lungs.

I fell to my knees and bent over, trying to stay on the ground, grasping at nothing but the carpet, but its tightly woven texture refused to give my desperate fingers any anchor. I felt the tor-nado beckoning me to itself. With nothing for me to hold on to and nothing holding on to me, I feared I would obey its inevitable call. Suddenly, a couch rammed up against my side and wedged my foot between it and the floor, followed by something that felt like a table falling on my back, as if to protect me and cover me from the raging storm. Seconds later, everything stopped and fell silent. I opened my eyes to see that a battery-powered emergency lamp had fallen a foot from my face, providing me light.

An F-4 tornado destroyed our campus the night of Febru-ary 5, 2008. I was trapped under rubble for two hours but later walked out of the hospital with only minor cuts and bruises. Even more miraculous, no one on our campus died. God was there that night, but He was not in the wind. He came in the soft, gentle whisper that continually tells us to hold on. He tells us to trust Him and take Him at His word.

Like the Casting Crowns song "Praise You in the Storm" says, "As the thunder rolls, I barely hear you whisper through the rain, 'I am with you.' And as your mercy falls, I raise my hands and praise the God who gives and takes away."

God speaks in the silence and through His whisper. Sometimes it just takes a tornado to hear Him.

Journal Response

The disciples went and woke him, saying, "Master, Master, we're going to drown!" He got up and rebuked the wind and the raging waters; the storm subsided, and all was calm. "Where is your faith?" he asked his disciples. In fear and amazement they asked another, "Who is this? He commands even the winds and the water, and they obey him."

LUKE 8:24-25

Whether we like it or not, we are going to face times of stress and anxiety. How is God using storms (literal or metaphorical ones) to speak to you? What may God be teaching you about faith through these frightening experiences?

_____

_____

_____

_____

_____

_____

_____

_____

Can You Hear Him?

By Annaruth Sarcone, Kean University

And after the earthquake a fire, but the LORD was not in the fire;
and after the fire a still small voice.
1 KINGS 19:12, *NKJV*

Alone in a mountain cave, the man huddled against a wall and questioned his sanity. He had not eaten for 40 days or nights, and a number of outraged people sought to kill him. Sitting in the dark, he waited. Suddenly, a great and strong wind came out of nowhere, tearing into the mountain and breaking rocks into pieces! The wind ceased and was briefly followed by an earthquake. To make matters worse, a large fire swept past his hideout, causing him to crawl even deeper into the cave. The fire stopped and the earth was silent. Then, soft and gentle, the voice of the Lord whispered to Elijah.

While I doubt any of us have ever encountered a situation similar to Elijah's, we have all faced obstacles and distractions that have kept us from hearing God's voice. As students, daily life can be just as loud as an earthquake or a howling wind. Midterms, finals, projects and papers are just some of the joys of college life. And, of course, there is always the end-of-semester crunch when all the professors try to squeeze 100 more things into our heads before we leave. Amidst all that noise, how can we hear His quiet voice?

While exploring my campus between classes, I discovered a hidden garden. It was a beautiful haven with colorful trees, flowers and a creek running through it. I sat on one of the benches and rummaged through my bag. Inside, I found a novel, my Bible and a notebook.

I decided to have a short devotional first and then kill the rest of the time with the novel. What I did not expect, however, was how absorbed I became in Psalm 23 as I sat beside literal green pastures and still waters. For the first time in my life, I spent four hours digging into one psalm, jotting down everything I learned from it. The result was 20 pages of new insights into a psalm I previously thought was very familiar. It was a very personal and exciting meeting with God. The difference was that this time, I let Him do all the talking.

How long has it been since you last heard His soft voice? Take time today to admire His creation and quiet your thoughts. He is whispering something. Can you hear Him?

Journal Response

The Lord is my shepherd; I shall not want. He maketh me to lie down in green pastures: he leadeth me beside the still waters. He restoreth my soul: he leadeth me in the paths of righteousness for his name's sake. Yea, though I walk through the valley of the shadow of death, I will fear no evil: for thou art with me; thy rod and thy staff they comfort me. Thou preparest a table before me in the presence of mine enemies: thou anointest my head with oil; my cup runneth over. Surely goodness and mercy shall follow me all the days of my life: and I will dwell in the house of the Lord for ever.

PSALM 23, *KJV*

Read this psalm aloud at least twice. What fresh insights or renewed comfort do you obtain from the images of Psalm 23? (Consider reading the psalm in another translation to give you additional perspective.)

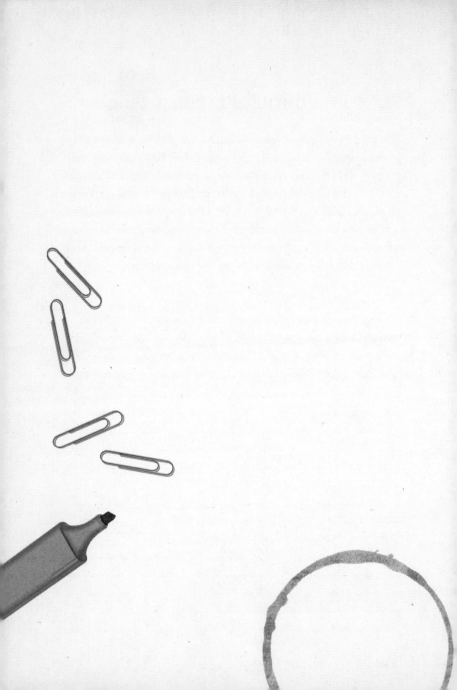

Part 3

Voices of Forgiveness and Encouragement

Do not let any unwholesome talk come out of your mouths, but only what is helpful for building others up according to their needs, that it may benefit those who listen. And do not grieve the Holy Spirit of God, with whom you were sealed for the day of redemption. Get rid of all bitterness, rage and anger, brawling and slander, along with every form of malice. Be kind and compassionate to one another, forgiving each other just as in Christ God forgave you.

EPHESIANS 4:29-32

To err is human; to forgive, divine.

ALEXANDER POPE

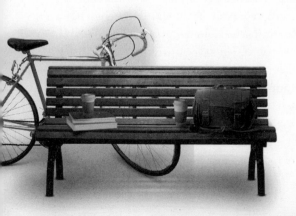

Forgiveness

By Nathan Fisher, Union University

For if you forgive people their wrongdoing,
your heavenly Father will forgive you as well.

MATTHEW 6:14, *HCSB*

Like many other Union University students before the tornado hit our campus, I took too much for granted. One thing that bothered me the night of the storm was that I was holding on to insignificant grudges that were potentially damaging—little things a roommate said, meaningless jokes and misinterpreted comments. I kept the resentment inside and never let it out. These hidden things weren't just eating away at me; they were eating away at my relationships as well.

That night, February 5, 2008, I realized I couldn't keep my bitterness inside any more. When everything that is important to you is almost ripped away, you see things in a different light. I sure did. I spoke to my friends and family as soon as possible. I told them I was sorry for whatever I had done or said that might have hurt them. I was truly sorry. I asked that they forgive me. I didn't want anything to come between us, and since that night nothing has.

Since I came to that realization, I have viewed my campus and my relationships differently. My housing complex is gone, but new things are to come—just like with relationships. The old feelings were swept away, and new feelings of friendship and community are filling the empty space. I felt something similar when I accepted the forgiveness and love of Jesus about five years ago.

This concept of forgiveness reminded me of the school shooting in West Paducah, Kentucky, back in 1997. The only reason I am familiar with the story is because I read the book *Run, Baby, Run* by Nicky Cruz. The edition I read (which I can't quote directly, due to the tornado) contained details about ministry work Nicky Cruz has done.

One event where he helped troubled teens was the school shooting in West Paducah. I won't go into detail, but a 14-year-old boy fired shots into a group of students praying before school one day. Five were injured; three were killed. When Cruz later interviewed a female student who was paralyzed for life after a bullet hit her spine, he asked her if she forgave the classmate who shot her. Her reply, the part I remember word for word, was, "With all my heart."

Everyone can take something from her example. I know I have. Few of us will ever have to forgive so horrible an act. So shouldn't forgiving others be easier for us?

Journal Response

Praise the Lord, O my soul; all my inmost being, praise his holy name.
Praise the Lord, O my soul, and forget not all his benefits—who forgives
all your sins and heals all your diseases, who redeems your life from the
pit and crowns you with love and compassion, who satisfies your desires
with good things so that your youth is renewed like the eagle's.

PSALM 103:1-5

Why is it sometimes hard to forgive? Think of a time when you received forgiveness for an intended or even an unintended transgression. What benefits, both personal and spiritual, did you obtain from experiencing forgiveness?

Door Number Two

By Kimberley Wilcox, Azusa Pacific University

How precious are your thoughts about me, O God.
They cannot be numbered!
PSALM 139:17, *NLT*

Have you ever noticed on game shows that the door the contestants select is always their final choice? Few game shows give contestants the opportunity to try another door or trade their prize for a better one.

That isn't how life works with God, though. If we allow God to choose our doors and listen to Him when making our decisions, He will lead us to the best door. Of course, getting to that door may require effort. We may have to retrace our steps and go back and choose the correct door the second time.

The summer of my freshman year in college, I needed a job. I applied everywhere. There was one position I thought would be perfect for me, and I wanted it so badly. It was like gold to me, and all I could do was pray that I got it. Well, I didn't. In fact, an employer from a place I had applied a month earlier eventually called and asked if I was still interested in working there. It was not my first choice, but I took the job. I am still working for that company. They give me great hours and work around my school schedule, and they are understanding about the fact that I will be leaving them as soon as I graduate.

God offered me door number two when I had so wanted door number one. He offered me a job that, by my standards, was not as great but by His standards worked perfectly into His plan. Because of my flexible job, I have since had the opportunity to be active at school, have a social life and attend church every Sunday.

I chose door number one, but God closed that door and opened number two, hoping that I would choose to follow Him. By doing so, everything else has just fallen into place.

What Are You Afraid of?

Have you ever been paralyzed by uncertainty when it comes to determining God's will? We sometimes fear failure or experience anxiety about following God perfectly. So what can we do when we prayerfully request a giant neon sign that will point us in the right direction, but the sign never lights up?

When you desire to please God but just aren't sure if an "open door" is the one you should enter, why not just go back to the BASICS?

Believe in God's plan for you (see Ephesians 2:8-10). You have been created for a purpose—one that was prearranged with you specifically in mind—to live for His glory. Believe that God has a plan for you.

Accept that God is sovereign and in control of all things (see Ecclesiastes 3:14). If God has a plan for you, do you have complete trust in that plan? You should! Trust that God actually can do what He promised.

Submit your will to the Lord (see Luke 9:23-24). Is there any area of your life that you have failed to surrender to God? Living the life of a disciple of Christ is a daily commitment to place your whole life in His hands. To submit means following Jesus even during times when circumstances don't make sense or you've been treated unfairly.

Imagine what God could do through you if you would only obey (see Ephesians 3:20-21). Now comes the fun part. You can experience a peace-filled life, knowing that you are serving a God who has empowered you to do amazing things for His glory. Go ahead—dream a little with God on what you can accomplish with and for Him.

Courageously pray for the attitude of the apostle Paul, who knew no limits in serving God (see Philippians 4:12-13). Sometimes, God's path is marked with warnings and limitations by secular standards. Nevertheless, take courage, for the God of all creation has prepared you for this very task.

Step out in faith, knowing that God loves you even in times of doubt, confusion and fear (see Romans 8:26-28). As you step out in faith, relax! What are you afraid of? Is anything impossible with God?

—Brian Benson, Talbot School of Theology

18

Guilt and Forgiveness

By Brent Godwin, Auburn University

Saving is all his idea, and all his work. All we do is trust him enough to let him do it. It's God's gift from start to finish!
EPHESIANS 2:8-9, *THE MESSAGE*

One of the things I struggle with most in my walk with the Lord is guilt. I became a Christian at a young age and grew up in church. For years I've sung songs about God's grace, about His forgiveness and the unconditional love He has for me. None of it made much sense until this year.

I had always heard about Christ making us "free of our sins." What? But I'm *not* free of sin; I still sin all the time! The Bible tells us that through Jesus we are no longer under control of our sinful nature, but for me that just made me feel guiltier every time I sinned. Every time I did something wrong, I spent the next few days, or even weeks, beating myself up over it—and feeling terrible that even though Christ died for me, I still sinned.

Going to church made me feel terrible, and, in general, I just felt separated from the Lord. I believed that Christ died for me and that I was forgiven, but for some reason that didn't make me feel better. If I fell into some kind of sin, I knew I needed to pray and confess it to Him. However, those prayers usually went something like this: "God, I'm sorry I sinned. I'm sorry. I'm sorry, I'm sorry, I'm so sorry . . ." I would just apologize until I felt better.

That is not what Christ had in mind when He washed us of all our sins by dying on the cross! When Christ died on the cross, all the work of forgiveness was finished. This means that forgiveness of our sins has nothing to do with how many times we apologize or how well we word our prayers of repentance. As Brennan Manning says in his book *Ragamuffin Gospel*, "Repentance is not what we do in order to earn forgiveness; it is what we do because we have been forgiven."

What I had never understood was *grace* and what it really means. Forgiveness was provided a long time before we ever sinned and then prayed to confess it! God doesn't even need an explanation of where we have been or what we have done. His grace is 100-percent free. God welcomes us back with open arms, just as the father did in the story of the Prodigal Son. The father didn't say, "Son, first of all, where did you go? What have you been doing?" The father was happy just to have the son back, and he clothed him with a robe and placed a ring on his finger. Our Father does the same when we come back to Him.

Journal Response

Therefore, there is now no condemnation for those who are in Christ Jesus, because through Christ Jesus the law of the Spirit of life set me free from the law of sin and death. For what the law was powerless to do in that it was weakened by the sinful nature, God did by sending his own Son in the likeness of sinful man to be a sin offering.

ROMANS 8:1-3

As a Christian, you have been set free from the law of sin and death. How can that knowledge liberate you from the burden of misplaced guilt or the frustration of repeated failures?

Evaluation

By Rebeckah M. Reader, Butler University

Put on then, as God's chosen ones, holy and beloved, compassionate hearts, kindness, humility, meekness, and patience, bearing with one another, and if one has a complaint against another, forgiving each other; as the Lord has forgiven you, so you also must forgive.
COLOSSIANS 3:12-13, ESV

"I am going to rip him apart." As I hung up the phone with my friend, I began to contemplate my course of action. It was professor evaluation day, and I had been looking forward to this day all semester. As soon as my professor handed out the syllabus, I began a running log of his every little infraction, annoyance and injustice.

This was not the first course I had been required to take with this particular professor. I began running through my log. My wicked smile grew as I recounted everything on my list— every unreturned email, every missed appointment, every 10-page paper proposal, every 25-page transcription assignment, every 7-page article, every obscure question on every exam, every 100-page chapter required, and every hour I listened to my professor drone on and on. I had logged it all away. The time had finally come to unload, and I was so pumped.

I may not have enjoyed every admonition I had received to be thorough in my news writing class, but I was going to enjoy being as thorough as possible in obliterating my professor. That would show him. As I was chuckling to myself about possibly needing more than one sheet of paper to do this evaluation justice, I heard a little voice admonish me for being so heartless.

I knew this little voice was the Holy Spirit. My smile turned to a frown as I realized how unforgiving and cruel I was being. The Lord opened my eyes to see my actions for what they really were and to see my professor as Christ did.

My anger and frustration over this course may have been justified, but it was not just for me to allow my emotions to block Christ's love from coming through.

The soft voice whispered, "Does he really deserve this?" I knew in my heart that my professor had earned and deserved my disdain. That had been my creed all semester. But I also knew in my heart that I deserved worse for my sins. Christ had forgiven and loved me. It was only right for me to do the same.

It seemed as though today was an evaluation day for me as well. Humbled, I asked for forgiveness and decided to try forgiving my professor.

> *And above all these put on love, which binds*
> *everything together in perfect harmony.*
> COLOSSIANS 3:14, ESV

Survival Guide for a Difficult Class

No matter how much you love university life or how hard you work, at some point in your college career, you will encounter a class you do not enjoy or a professor who irritates you. Here's some advice that may help you survive that complication.

Remember that classes run for a limited number of weeks. You must endure only for a time.

Consider that professors are people too. Pray for them, even the ones you don't like.

Recognize the professor's strengths even if they're not yours. Appreciate the individual differences in your professors.

Keep a good attitude—you will get more flies with honey than with vinegar.

Don't be afraid of a challenge; view the class as a test, not a trial.

Dealing with a difficult professor may prepare you for the future—like dealing with a boss you don't care for.

Ponder the drop option. You are in the driver's seat and can choose to opt out of a course.

Remember that you're not the center of the universe. Consider viewpoints other than your own.

Don't forget the Golden Rule. Be respectful and kind.

Even if you think you are brighter than the professor, keep in mind that the professor can still teach you something.

Distinguish between the subject matter and the professor—maybe it's the subject matter that you really don't like.

Join classmates in taking a professor to lunch and get him or her to talk about his or her field of study. Perhaps that informal environment will provide an even better learning experience.

—Michelle Williams, Biola University

20

Wake Up!

By Mandy McCullough, Belhaven College

Restore to me the joy of Your salvation and uphold me with a willing spirit.
PSALM 51:12, *AMP*

A few Sundays ago, four of my college friends came to visit my church. The pastor preached about how true revival starts in each Christian's heart. I thought it was very interesting and listened intently. However, when I looked at the girl sitting next to me, I noticed she had fallen asleep.

I became very indignant. How dare she come to *my* church and fall asleep in *my* service? I kept glancing over at her, and each time I became more and more agitated. I completely stopped listening to the message and just seethed over her lack of interest.

I tried to think of reasonable excuses for her being tired. Maybe she hadn't been feeling well and had been unable to sleep. What if she stayed up late counseling an upset friend? Then all of a sudden, out of nowhere, I heard a small voice. *"So what* if you can stay awake for a sermon when you're asleep the rest of the week." *What?* I knew it was a thought from God but couldn't make sense of it. Yet the more I considered it, the clearer it became.

David wrote Psalm 51 after he had an affair with Bathsheba and had her husband killed. Within the psalm, he cries out to God, asking for forgiveness and mercy. While most college students haven't been involved in adulterous affairs or committed murder, we're like David. He ignored God to gain his own desires. In our everyday lives, we often get so wrapped up in our busyness that we ignore God. We are spiritually asleep to His voice.

Like David, we have lost the joy of salvation. While being busy with exams, papers and projects isn't a sin, when busyness causes us to become numb to God's voice, it becomes sinful. This is exactly what happened to me this year. Even though I was attending a Christian college and talking every day in class about having a Christian worldview, I stopped listening to God. I lost the joy of my salvation and fell asleep to God's voice.

Luckily, God forgives us. Psalm 23:3 says, "He refreshes and restores my life" (*AMP*). So if life's busyness has robbed you of your joy, take a moment to ask for forgiveness. Then rejoice, "For the Lord is good and his love endures forever; his faithfulness continues through all generations" (Psalm 100:5).

Journal Response

You are forgiving and good, O Lord, abounding in love to all who call to you. Hear my prayer, O Lord; listen to my cry for mercy. In the day of my trouble I will call to you, for you will answer me.

PSALM 86:5-7

How has your busy schedule deafened God's voice recently? In what ways could you wake up to the reality of God's love and care for you? How will you give your attention to God's leading and direction?

_____

_____

_____

_____

21

When Coffee Isn't Enough

By Katie Dudgeon, Talbot School of Theology

And we urge you, brothers, admonish the idle, encourage the fainthearted, help the weak, be patient with them all.
1 Thessalonians 5:14, *esv*

A lot of people love mornings. They love getting up early or sneaking in a quick workout before the rest of the world wakes up. I am not one of those people. I need time to take the world in with a cup of coffee in one hand and my Bible in the other.

My first year of seminary, though, I was forced to take a Greek grammar class at 7:30 in the morning. I knew it wasn't a good idea, but I couldn't have foreseen how bad an idea it was! I struggled to stay awake in class, and even a quart of coffee didn't help. I kept up with the reading, but I got Cs on the quizzes and almost failed the midterm.

I knew I wouldn't pass the class if I didn't improve my grade drastically, so I made an intentional effort to meet with my professor outside class and be part of a study group. Thankfully, my professor willingly spent hours helping struggling students like me. Aaron, a classmate, helped me review Greek vocabulary as we sped down the freeway, carpooling to class in the mornings. Both Aaron and my professor generously spent their time outside class helping me prepare for papers and tests, in addition to their own heavy workloads.

Although detailed grammatical analysis of a dead language is not something I am innately gifted at, I began to see the fruit of my hard work and the benefits of being a diligent student of God's Word. The skills and tools I developed in class were important, but even more significant was the opportunity to see God's faithfulness that semester. God used my professor and my friend to challenge me and support me when I was discouraged and, frankly, wanted to burn my "Big Fat Greek" textbook.

The apostle Paul was intentional about challenging the Thessalonians to encourage one another to persevere and show each other love. In 1 Thessalonians 5:11, Paul says, "Therefore encourage one another and build each other up, just as you are doing" (*ESV*). He gives them specific ways to encourage one another: "admonish the idle, encourage the fainthearted, help the weak, and be patient with them all" (v. 14, *ESV*).

Have we been recipients of godly encouragement? Let's take a minute to think about others we know who admonish us, serve us or are patient with us—especially in the midst of a challenge. Thank God for the blessing and encouragement they are, and ask Him to help each of us "increase and abound in love for one another" (1 Thessalonians 3:12, *ESV*).

How to Find Some Study Buddies

Perhaps you're in one of those general education classes that just doesn't match your academic aptitudes, or you're struggling in that statistics class you need for your major, but the numbers just don't add up. That's the time to consider finding or forming a student study group. Here are a few tips for creating a successful one.

Seek other students in the class who, like you, are motivated to succeed. Willingly include different personality types.

Set a consistent time and location to meet each week. Respect the time commitments of the group members. Don't be late.

Find students who possess different learning styles and abilities, like good note takers, creative thinkers, questioners and effective communicators.

Limit the number of group members. You should have more than 3 but less than 10.

Be sure that each member has a chance to participate in discussion. One or two students should not dominate the group's conversation. Designate a leader who will keep the discussion moving forward.

Take responsibility for communicating concepts to other group members. Those who explain material to others will learn more themselves. Be willing to share notes, anticipate test questions and reinforce material covered in class.

Be sure that each session is productive. Set goals. Evaluate progress. Don't let the sessions devolve into a social event.

Ask your professor for advice on strategies for learning the course material.

The Call

By Bret Burchard, Taylor University

Many, O Lord my God, are the wonders you have done.
The things you planned for us no one can recount to you;
were I to speak and tell of them, they would be too many to declare. . . .
I desire to do your will, O my God; your law is within my heart.

PSALM 40:5,8

In Christian circles, we are always talking about hearing God's call and figuring out God's will for our lives and His purpose for us. This is especially true in college when we are trying to decide what our majors will be or what we're going to do after graduation. We read all these books that tell us how to find God's will for us and how we can know if it's what we're called to do.

I don't think we're supposed to know completely what God's will or plan is for our lives. If we knew, it would become—or we would make it—our plan, and we'd probably mess it up. I think God's call is simple: to live today, right now, faithfully and righteously. Given what we know—the extent of our wisdom—we should live today the best we possibly can. We should live by His teachings. We should live with integrity and honesty. We should treat people right. Our call is to be a disciple today.

That's the call. So, what are we supposed to do? What are we supposed to major in? Where are we supposed to work? I believe God is our creator. And not just physically—He created our emotions, our interests and our passions. If we want to know where

God is calling us to work or what we're supposed to do, we should just follow our passions and interests. We should examine our strengths. They are gifts from God. We should follow those strengths and use them to the best of our ability. We should do something that we can give our whole selves to—something that challenges and charges us up. Not something we do half-heartedly (even if we do it well), but something we give our whole hearts to, because we are supposed to serve the Lord with our whole hearts.

The call is to be a daily disciple. Where we go from there is not our decision. If we follow our passions and interests and strengths, the Lord's plans will evolve as they are supposed to.

Journal Response

As Jesus walked beside the Sea of Galilee, he saw Simon and his brother Andrew casting a net into the lake, for they were fishermen. "Come, follow me," Jesus said, "and I will make you fishers of men." At once they left their nets and followed him.

MARK 1:16-18

What does being Christ's disciple mean to you? How do you live out that concept? In what ways is following Christ sometimes easy and sometimes difficult?

_____

_____

_____

_____

_____

_____

Twice as Much

By Courtney Jo Veasey, New Orleans Baptist Theological Seminary

*Return to your fortress, O prisoners of hope; even now I announce
that I will restore twice as much to you.*

ZECHARIAH 9:12

When Hurricane Katrina hit New Orleans only three weeks after I moved there, I was forced to return home to Florida and live temporarily with my dad. Aside from the truck I drove home in and the jeans and sweatshirt I had on when I left, almost all my personal belongings were lost in the storm. I was devastated. But as I sought the Lord, He brought me to this verse in Zechariah as my anthem.

In the time of Zechariah the prophet, God's children were brought out of captivity and encouraged to return to their fortress of Jerusalem. God promised that there He would restore twice as much as they had before. I asked God, "Is my Florida hometown the 'fortress' for me? Or is New Orleans the 'fortress' where You will return to me more than what I lost?"

In time, my heavenly Father showed me that the real "fortress" He wanted me to return to and abide in during that difficult time was His Son, Jesus. I put my trust in Christ, and He not only returned tangible possessions to me but also taught me "twice as much" as I knew before about His love and sovereign control over my life. During that year of being home, my dad began to attend church and become a more committed Christian.

My sister, who also lived close by, put both my niece and nephew in Christian schools. Not only did my family finally come around to Christianity, but we also became closer.

As far as "tangible things" were concerned, God blessed me over and abundantly. I learned that Jesus was all I needed and that I could do without half the stuff I had before Katrina. I lost all my personal possessions, but my family, friends, church groups and other organizations showered me with gift cards, money, clothes, new Bibles and textbooks—until all my belongings had been replaced (and all brand new!).

One day not long after the hurricane, I went to a consignment store, trying to make the best use of the money I had been given to replace my entire wardrobe. I had been sulking with the Lord on the way there, praying for encouragement. After a few minutes in the store, I looked up on a display shelf and saw a purse there—exactly like one I had lost in the storm. It had been my favorite for years! When I took it up to the counter, the saleswoman said, "I knew I should have put this one away for myself when it came in! We just put it out." It made me smile because it reminded me that God, my Fortress, cared intimately about every detail of my life, down to the smallest, silliest thing, like a purse I loved.

Hurricane Facts

Hurricanes and typhoons are cyclones. Typhoons occur in the Northwest Pacific Ocean west of the international dateline, while hurricanes develop in the North Atlantic and Northeast Pacific Oceans east of the dateline. These storms develop over warm tropical oceans. Fueled by thunderstorms and evaporating seawater, the system moves counter-clockwise with winds of 75 mph or higher. The most severe storms are designated as Category Five, with winds greater than 155 mph.

Hurricane season extends from August to October, although it is possible for hurricanes to occur anytime between June and November. These powerful storms force water toward shorelines. Combined with the tide, these "storm surges" can raise coastal water levels by more than 15 feet. The intense winds and floods produce a great deal of damage once the hurricanes reach land.

Here is a list of some of America's most powerful hurricanes:

Camille (1969)—Category 5: 335 deaths and more than 22,000 homes destroyed

Hugo (1989)—Category 4: 26 deaths and more than 5,000 homes destroyed

Andrew (1992)—Category 5: 61 deaths and more than 79,000 homes destroyed

Ivan (2004)—Category 3: 57 deaths and more than 27,000 homes destroyed

Katrina (2005)—Category 3: 1,330 deaths and more than 200,000 homes destroyed[1]

Note

1. *Florida Division of Emergency Management,* http://www.floridadisaster.org; "Hurricanes," *FEMA for Kids,* http://www.fema.gov/kids/hurr.htm; "Hurricane Research Division: Frequently Asked Questions," *Atlantic Oceanographic and Meteorological Research,* http://www.aoml.noaa.gov/hrd/tcfaq/A1.html; "Hurricane Hugo," *NOAA Coastal Services Center,* http://www.csc.noaa.gov; "Chapter One: Katrina in Perspective," http://www.whitehouse.gov/reports/katrina-lessons-learned/chapter1.html; "Hurricane Research Division," *Atlantic Oceanographic and Meteorological Laboratory,* http://www.aoml.noaa.gov/hrd.

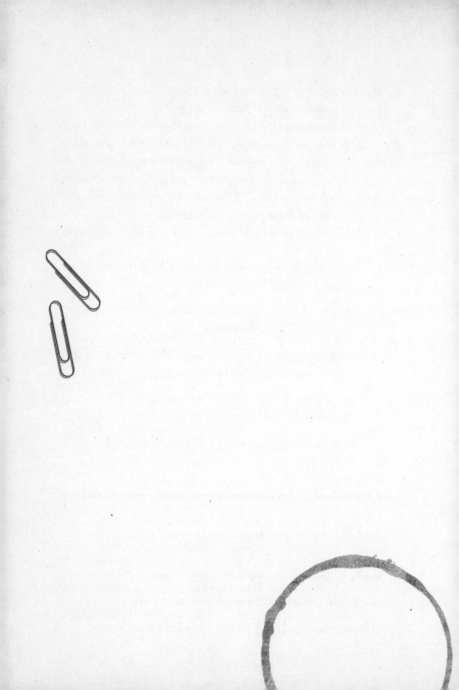

Part 4

Voices of Identity and Personality

For you created my inmost being; you knit me together in my mother's womb. I praise you because I am fearfully and wonderfully made; your works are wonderful, I know that full well. My frame was not hidden from you when I was made in the secret place. When I was woven together in the depths of the earth, your eyes saw my unformed body. All the days ordained for me were written in your book before one of them came to be. How precious to me are your thoughts, O God!

PSALM 139:13-17

The way to gain a good reputation is to endeavor to be what you desire to appear.

SOCRATES

Valer la Pena

By Christine Baumgartner, Biola University

*But a poor widow came and put in two very small copper coins,
worth only a fraction of a penny.*
MARK 12:42

Valer la pena is a Spanish expression that means "to be worthwhile." It translates literally into "to be worth pain or grief." I learned the phrase one morning in Spanish class and thought about it the rest of the day. How many times do I really hear that I'm worthwhile? I mean, I know I'm not worthless. I'm occasionally complimented on how I look on a particular day, or I earn good grades for doing well on a particular assignment. Though looking good or performing well academically gives me confidence, it's a little harder to believe I'm worth someone else's grief or pain.

Throughout elementary and high school, my self-worth was attacked in subtle ways. People I hung out with merely *allowed* me to tag along. They didn't seek my company or confide in me. I wasn't worthy of even being told they didn't want me around. I was the tolerated companion. I've experienced this "fringe" feeling at home, too. My younger siblings have far more active social lives than I do. When I'm home for weekend visits, my brother and sister are often so busy with friends they don't have much time for me.

Not long ago, one of my friends called to say he'd make the six-hour drive from his home to visit me at school. "I'll come after work on Friday," he told me, "but I'll have to leave Saturday night so I can be back home for church on Sunday morning."

"That's too much trouble," I told him. "You don't have to drive all that way for just one day."

"Hey," he said, "you're worth it."

Me? Worth someone else's pain and trouble and lack of sleep? Am I really?

I can open my Bible and find numerous examples of God's love for other "fringe people" like me. Take Leah, for example. Leah, the first, unwanted wife of Jacob. Because God saw that Jacob did not want Leah, He gave her children—many children. She learned to seek her worth in God and praise Him.

The greatest example of our worthiness is exemplified in Jesus' death on the cross. Why else would He bother, if it weren't for us? God affirms that we are worth pain, grief and trouble. Jesus showed that our future is worthy of His death. We can be confident that God finds us worthy.

What can be seen as worthless by many people, like the poor widow's two tiny copper coins, can be of great worth in God's eyes. Jesus sees great value in us and in anything we have to offer Him.

Valo la pena, vales la pena. I am worthwhile, and so are you.

It's All About Me

University life brings together many different types of people. Living in close quarters forces us to be more aware of the needs of others, even those we don't always understand. However, when difficulties arise at school, students can become so over-whelmed by circumstances that they focus only on their own problems. Every once in a while, everyone needs a reality check to curb his or her selfish tendencies.

Here are some ways to tell when you are becoming too self-centered:

You gaze at your reflection in every mirror, window or pond you pass.

Every sentence you speak begins with the word "I."

Your Facebook page features 100 photos of you.

You buy a gift for a sick friend and then decide to keep it for yourself and just pray that the friend feels better soon.

You know you deserve to be first in line.

You always arrive late and leave early.

You idolize Miss Piggy and Donald Trump.

You drink your roommate's orange juice out of the carton.

You take all calls on your cell phone, no matter where you happen to be.

Your favorite iPod tune is Carly Simon's "You're So Vain."

You never give up your seat on a bus, plane, train, airport waiting area or other public location.

You wear your roommates' clothes without permission.

You hitch rides with your various friends but never offer to pay for gas.

Your favorite expression is, "It's my way or the highway."

You feel the need to carve your name into classroom tables and dorm room desks.

You think Apple has named all their products after you: iPhone, iChat, iPod, iTunes.

You think you're the one exception to the verse, "For all have sinned . . ."

> *Do nothing out of selfish ambition or vain conceit,*
> *but in humility consider others better than yourselves.*
> PHILIPPIANS 2:3

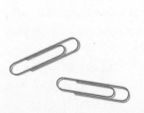

25

Shattered Mirrors

By Jennifer Campbell, Azusa Pacific University

Now we see but a poor reflection as in a mirror;
then we shall see face to face. Now I know in part; then I shall
know fully, even as I am fully known.
1 CORINTHIANS 13:12

Now we see but a poor reflection as in a mirror. Candlelight gently glowed around me in the darkness of a prayer tent that was furnished with a red carpet and a gold-framed mirror. In the silent pause between tearful gasps, I lifted my eyes from the ground and caught a glimpse of an unfamiliar and terrifying sight: A bleached-white face, unnaturally inflamed eyes and twisted mouth loomed before me in the mirror. Like a movie villain, my contorted physical appearance mirrored my poisoned spirit. Repulsed by the skeletal image, my eyes fell back to the ground.

Then we shall see face to face. "Who are you?" was the theme question at this year's retreat. An easy question to answer: "I am Jen, the straight-*A* student, dedicated gymnast, caring friend and pastor's kid." At least that's who I saw staring back at me every time I did my hair in the morning. That's who the world's mirrors reflected, because grades, athleticism, acquaintances and family defined every part of me.

Now I know in part. The mirror gives a poor reflection of what's going on inside me. It never fails to show what I look like on the outside, good-hair or bad-acne day, but it rarely ever shows who I am on the inside. It fails to know who I am. The tent isolated me from the definitions imposed by my professors, coaches and friends. Now, I was forced to face the skeletal image of myself. I looked at the reflection God saw. It wasn't pretty. I was a shell of meaningless, worldly "good looks."

Then I shall know fully. Yet, in that vulnerable moment, God asked to take the worldly reflection and make me undefined. He doesn't want me to look in the mirror and see only a student or gymnast. He wants me to see what He sees: His child.

Even as I am fully known. By surrendering all the distortions that glare back, God shatters the artificial mirrors, leaving only the image He knows inside and out. Take time with a journal and coffee away from the things that easily define who you are and pray for God to show you who He sees.

Journal Response

Search me, O God, and know my heart . . . see if there is any offensive way in me, and lead me in the way everlasting.
PSALM 139:23-24

What spiritual struggles are you currently experiencing? What comfort can you find in being still and listening for God's voice?

_____

_____

_____

_____

_____

26

Being My Own Person

By Lauren E. Gossett, Point Loma Nazarene University

*Trust in the LORD with all of your heart and lean not on
your own understanding; in all your ways acknowledge him,
and he will make your paths straight.*

PROVERBS 3:5-6

I vividly remember so many starry-eyed moments from my freshman year of college: a trail of roses leading up to my room, kayaking in the ocean at sunset, and bike riding to the nearby pier for lunch. For some girls these images seem romantic and ideal in a relationship, but I found these sweetly intended gestures over the top and a little uncomfortable. But the sighs of appreciation from so many of the girls in my hall convinced me to accept the flowers and ignore my discomfort. I was caught up in what I thought was a great and healthy relationship, but after a while I realized a major change had taken place in me.

My life began to revolve around this one guy, and every time my girlfriends wanted to hang out with me or go out to dinner, I found myself checking not only *my* schedule but *his* as well to make sure he and I didn't already have plans. I ditched my friends so that I could be with this guy at every possible moment. I was no longer the carefree individual I had been at the beginning of my freshman year; I was now so entirely wrapped up in a relationship that I had lost my own identity.

People around campus began to recognize me as so-and-so's girlfriend; I was hardly ever recognized by my own name. When the relationship ended, I realized it had been founded on my desire to be wanted. Having never been in a relationship before, I had craved the attention that was suddenly directed my way, and I didn't seek the Lord's guidance on how to proceed. I neglected to ask the Lord to guide my path, and I didn't trust Him enough to believe that one day He would place me in a healthy relationship founded on a mutual love in Him.

If you can't be your own person outside of a relationship, then there is no chance of you finding yourself or being yourself *in* one. The only way to become and to do what you are meant to do is to "trust in the Lord with all of your heart."

Relationships

Success in relationships requires that couples engage in effective communication, have a firm sense of commitment as Christian believers, and possess a spirit of cooperation and mutual respect. Married men and women have to leave space for the other's development so that both personalities thrive. One person should not dominate the relationship. Here's a list of famous couples whose enduring marriages reflected the benefits of mutual respect and commitment.

John and Abigail Adams

John and Abigail were married on October 25, 1764. They survived the American Revolution, the War of 1812, the death of children and long separations while John served in the Continental Congress and in France as a diplomat. Despite these difficulties, the couple continually supported one another and often communicated through letters. Abigail served as John's confidante and advisor when he was president (1796–1800). They were married for 54 years.[1]

Harry and Bess Truman

The Trumans met in Missouri and were married on June 28, 1919. Bess helped her husband in his haberdashery (men's clothing) business before he entered politics. Harry Truman later served in Congress and became Franklin Roosevelt's vice president. When FDR died in office in 1945, Truman assumed the presidency. Throughout his political career, Bess willingly assumed the role of First Lady. She was known for her thoughtfulness, her understanding of protocol and her attention to detail. When the Trumans left the White House in 1953, they resumed a quiet life back in Missouri where they lived on the money Bess had saved. Their marriage lasted 53 years.[2]

Billy and Ruth Graham

Billy and Ruth Graham met while attending Wheaton College. They married on August 13, 1943. Ruth's parents were missionaries in China. When her evangelist husband was away on ministry trips, Ruth carried on her own ministry efforts while also rearing their children and managing the Graham household. Despite difficulties and times of separation, the couple remained devoted to one another until Ruth's death in 2007. They had been married 63 years.[3]

Paul Newman and Joanne Woodward

These actors met while in New York City in the early 1950s and married a few years later in Las Vegas on January 29, 1958. Both were Academy Award winners: Newman for *The Color of Money* (1986) and Woodward for *The Three Faces of Eve* (1957). The couple settled in Connecticut rather than Hollywood. Despite the pressures of movie careers and celebrity status, the couple had been married for 50 years when Paul died in September 2008.[4]

Notes

1. "American Experience: John and Abigail Adams," *PBS Online.* http://www.pbs.org.

2. "Harry S. Truman: American Visionary," U.S. Department of Interior National Park Service Museum Collections. http://www.nps.gov/history/museum/exhibits/hstr/.

3. "Ruth Graham, Soulmate to Billy, Dies," June 14, 2007, *Time Inc.* http://www.time.com/time/nation/article/0,8599,1633197,00.html; Marshall Shelley, "Ruth Graham Dies at 87," June 14, 2007, *Christianity Today.* http://www.christianitytoday.com/ct/2007/juneweb-only/124-43.0.html.

4. Sheri and Bob Stritof, "Paul Newman and Joanne Woodward Marriage Profile," *About.com.* http://marriage.about.com/od/entertainmen1/p/paulnewman.htm.

27

ABC

By Lynette Woo, Biola University

*This righteousness from God comes through faith in Jesus Christ
to all who believe. There is no difference, for all have sinned and fall short
of the glory of God, and all are justified freely by his grace through
the redemption that came by Christ Jesus.*

ROMANS 3:22-24

"*A* is for *Asian. B* is for *Better start studying so you can get an* A!"
So funny—yet so true. That's part of the experience of being a
Chinese kid growing up in America.

I've always had mixed feelings about being an ABC—American Born Chinese. Sometimes I feel ashamed. Other times I
want to be the perfect ABC. Either way, I've always felt stuck in
the middle. The way my mother describes it, "You're like a *jok
sing* [bamboo], not open either end." What she means is: we're
neither Chinese nor American; we don't really belong to one culture or the other.

In high school, it suddenly dawned on me that I was not
Chinese enough. I couldn't speak Cantonese, Mandarin or my
parents' regional Toisan dialect. I wasn't even sure if I pronounced
my name correctly. My inability to speak Chinese has been a constant source of embarrassment for me. Even now at Chinese
restaurants, waiters automatically speak to me in Chinese because, well, I look Chinese. Their questions go on until my face

turns red enough to indicate that I can't understand them. The little Chinese I know I'm scared to use because I don't want anyone to make fun of *my* accent.

To make up for my un-Chineseness, I always felt obligated to be the "perfect Asian kid." That meant no 99 percents on exams, no A-minuses on my report cards, and proficiency with at least one classical instrument. I carried this perfectionism with me through high school. However, when I entered college, I realized that getting good grades wasn't sufficient to make me Chinese. And straight As didn't give me true value or lasting satisfaction. The revelation I stumbled upon was simple: It really isn't necessary to calculate what percentage Chinese or what percentage American I am. Who I am in relation to God is far more important than being either Chinese or American.

In His sovereignty, God sent me to Hong Kong on a short-term missions trip. There He showed me that even though I couldn't speak Cantonese, He could use my proficiency in English, my passion for travel, my love of Chinese food and my connection to fellow students to minister to the young people I met in Hong Kong. God claimed my identity as a Chinese-American Christian student and used it for His purposes.

Our identity in Christ, especially as college students, should distinguish us more than anything else—more than race, ethnicity, background or personality. Those various qualities are all a part of how God made us. He wants to claim every aspect of who we are for His own glory. He wants to claim our schoolwork, our relationships and even our seemingly miscellaneous interests.

We can use the best facets from the different cultures we belong to—all those things that measure up to the Bible's standards for what is good and profitable for us. We must measure our culture against the truth of God's Word and conform our culture to Christ's rule. As my mom likes to remind me, I may be Chinese and I may be American, but I'm first and foremost a Christian, saved by grace through faith in Jesus Christ.

Journal Response

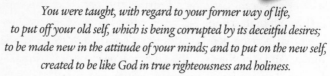

You were taught, with regard to your former way of life,
to put off your old self, which is being corrupted by its deceitful desires;
to be made new in the attitude of your minds; and to put on the new self,
created to be like God in true righteousness and holiness.

EPHESIANS 4:22-24

Part of the process of putting on a "new self" in Christ involves confronting social expectations. Everyone has expectations—our parents, professors, boyfriends or girlfriends. In what ways do you feel pressure to please others or conform to a certain social standard? How can an awareness of your identity in Christ free you from trying to satisfy the unrealistic expectations of others?

_____

_____

_____

_____

_____

_____

_____

_____

_____

_____

_____

_____

28

Beauty in Failure

By Kristyn Marie Johnson, Corban College

When I came to you, brothers, I did not come with eloquence or
superior wisdom as I proclaimed to you the testimony about God....
My message and my preaching were not with wise and persuasive words,
but with a demonstration of the Spirit's power, so that your faith
might not rest on men's wisdom, but on God's power.
1 CORINTHIANS 2:1,4-5

No matter how hard I try, I cannot get rid of my fear of failure.
I've sat in my dorm room for countless nights, mornings and
even afternoons, thinking about where I'm going in life. The moment I feel I'm finally on the right track—that I've found my direction—something happens to tear me down. The goals I'm
working toward go unmet, and that scary word comes up again:
failure. My best just wasn't good enough.

In my spirit, sanity and melancholy collide, and I realize
there's something I need to fix beyond mental motivation: I
need to fix my spiritual pace with Christ. I tend to either sprint
way ahead of God, thinking that I can handle life on my own, or
I slowly jog behind Him, having no desire to keep up. When failure knocks me down faster than I can get up, I'm suddenly reminded how important it is to stay side by side with Him. Only
then do I remember that God views me as something worth so
much more than I could imagine.

The beauty I have found in my failure is that in those moments of weakness and vulnerability, God's strength is beyond anything I could gain for myself. His overwhelming love, mercy and grace take my very breath away. The mere fact that He knows I will fail but will be there to pick me up still amazes me.

In Romans, Paul tells us that God feels our pain in our times of weakness. In fact, God probably grasps the experience of pain better than anyone else ever could. Not only does He understand rejection, ridicule, hatred and despair, but He also had to give up something priceless for us: His Son. When He watched His Son die on a cross for us, no one understood the pain He felt.

Nor will we fully understand why God puts us through the difficulties we experience in life. But—in the midst of our disappointments, our pain and our suffering—we feel His Spirit all around us. When we're reeling from failure and words fail us, He comprehends our feelings better than we ever could.

If you have made mistakes, even serious ones, there is always another chance for you. What we call failure is not in the falling down but in the staying down.
MARY PICKFORD

Failure and Success

Here are some thoughts about failure and success from those who know something about them.

"There is much to be said for failure. It is more interesting than success." —Max Beerbohm

"Success is a state of mind. If you want success, start thinking of yourself as a success." —Joyce Brothers

"Success is not final, failure is not fatal: it is the courage to continue that counts." —Sir Winston Churchill

"I have not failed. I've just found 10,000 ways that don't work." —Thomas Alva Edison

"Try not to become a man of success, but rather try to become a man of value." —Albert Einstein

"Your own resolution to succeed is more important than any one thing." —Abraham Lincoln

"Success usually comes to those who are too busy to be looking for it." —Henry David Thoreau

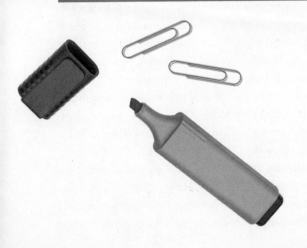

29

A Handful of Quietness

By Elise Toedt, Bethel University

*Better is a handful of quietness than two hands full
of toil and striving after wind.*
ECCLESIASTES 4:6, *ESV*

Professors read over my résumé in an Education Department entrance interview. Comments go something like this: "Oh, yes, the long-term involvement in a city outreach program looks good. Yes, and starting a club, great idea. Are you going to go overseas soon? Oh, I see, in the fall—good. And the library job, that's a plus."

While I appreciated the encouragement and the intent behind it, I also had a sinking feeling in my stomach. What does it mean if I work with people infected with HIV/AIDS merely to list it on a job application, or if I go abroad merely to show that I am globally minded? I constantly must question whether my motive is to reach an end rooted in a love of self or a genuine love for others. It is very easy to keep busy doing good things. But to reform one's mind so that outer actions reflect pure inner motives—that is a task.

Etched in black on my bedroom door are these lines from T. S. Eliot's "The Rock": "I say to you: *Make perfect your will.* I say: take no thought of the harvest, but only to proper sowing." In a world where knowledge (specifically at the university level) is becoming a lucrative commodity, the primary questions for me as a Christian are not necessarily what I am going to do with my education and what I need to do to get there, but who I am going to be while I'm learning and who I am going to be with what I have learned. I have the opportunity to be more than an intellectual person; I can take this gift and creatively use it to love my neighbors. Praying, "Thank You, Lord, for the opportunity of education," is not where my prayer should end. The prayer of gratefulness never ends. It translates into eagerly seeking opportunities to use my education in a hurting society.

Living my day among simple prayers like "God be near" and "Lord, have mercy" has taught me that life is a ripening process. I need time to evaluate and meditate on what is essential in life. I need time to realize every day that there is hope in the world and a purpose for each individual—a hope that cannot be summarized on a job application.

Traveling to the U.K. and to Africa, making genuine friends, doing interesting academic projects, being part of clubs—none of this has shaped my college experience like time to be still.

Journal Response

This is a large work I've called you into, but don't be overwhelmed by it. It's best to start small. Give a cool cup of water to someone who is thirsty, for instance. The smallest act of giving or receiving makes you a true apprentice. You won't lose out on a thing.

MATTHEW 10:41-42, *THE MESSAGE*

Sometimes we walk around with our eyes closed to the needs of others. If you open your eyes wide today, what small acts of service could you perform to help someone in a "hurting society"?

_____

_____

_____

_____

_____

_____

_____

_____

_____

_____

_____

_____

_____

_____

_____

_____

_____

When My Best Isn't Good Enough

By Rebekah Cooper, Biola University

*Are not two sparrows sold for a penny? Yet not one of them will
fall to the ground apart from the will of your Father. And even the
very hairs of your head are all numbered. So don't be afraid;
you are worth more than many sparrows.*

MATTHEW 10:29-31

I recently auditioned for the show *High School Musical: Get in the
Picture*. The show is a lot like *American Idol* in that you sing in
front of a judge and if you pass you go on to the next round.
I spent weeks preparing my songs, along with clever things to
say during my initial interview. After an agonizing two days of
waiting in lines, registering and sizing up the competition, my
turn finally came. Before I even stood to face the judge, I was a
bundle of nerves, which never bodes well for me. Sure enough,
my first song was a disaster, and the second one was not much
better. Needless to say, I was not asked to come back for the next
round of auditions.

Rejection hurts, and before I knew it, I was wondering if I
should change my major from theater to some other field. Perhaps the judges were right in not picking me; maybe I just
wasn't as good as I thought I was. Then I realized that I had

been looking for approval from other people and, when I didn't get it, I let it affect how I viewed myself. I had to remember that my worth comes through the Lord and that I am of infinite value to Him. Thankfully, God's love is unconditional and not based on performance.

Auditioning can be tricky. Whether you get the part or not, it's easy to forget God in the process. When you put yourself out there, only to have the casting director tell you that you aren't what they're looking for, it can be hard on the ego. When your self-esteem is at its lowest, Satan is at his strongest. He loves to make you think your value is based on other people's perceptions.

As an aspiring actress, I will always have people telling me no, but I can't let that rejection define me. So the next time I audition, I will remember to be thankful for the value God places on me whether I get the part or not!

Television Talent Shows

The talent show has long been a part of American television. The tradition began long before *American Idol*. It seems, these days, there's no end to the possibilities. If you have some peculiar talent, there might be a spot in the limelight just for you.

Talent Shows from the Past

Ted Mack's Original Amateur Hour, 1948–1970: Viewers voted for their favorite performers by mailing in postcards.

Arthur Godfrey's Talent Scouts, 1948–1958: Contestants performed for a studio audience. The winners were determined by measuring the audience's response on an "applause meter."

The Gong Show, 1976–1980: Chuck Barris hosted this irreverent talent show that sent weak performers away by sounding a gong. Contestants who escaped the gong were rated on a 1-10 scale by celebrity judges.

Talent Shows of the Present

A list of recent talent shows illustrates that reality television today has something for just about everyone:

Cooking: *Iron Chef; Top Chef; Hell's Kitchen*

Dancing: *So You Think You Can Dance; Dancing with the Stars*

Designing: *Design Star*

Entertaining: *America's Got Talent; Last Comic Standing*

Fashion: *Project Runway*

Heroism and strength: *Who Wants to Be a Superhero; Master of Champions*

Inventing: *American Inventor*

Modeling: *America's Next Top Model*

Singing: *American Idol; Rock Star*

Just As I Am

By Kristen Lynn Sadler, Biola University

[Your beauty] should be that of your inner self, the unfading beauty of a gentle and quiet spirit, which is of great worth in God's sight.

1 PETER 3:4

"Why are you so quiet . . . don't you have anything to add?"

"I'm doing this project for a class where I can't talk for 24 hours straight; kind of like what Kristen does all the time."

"Man, you never stop talking do you, Kristen?"

Some people who only partly know me would say I am quiet or reserved. My close friends and family would acknowledge that, too, but they also see my crazy side. The social demands of college, in and out of the classroom, have led me to reflect on my personality and to see how God has created me. I have always thought that being a quieter, calmer person was just not cool. I wanted to be outgoing, out there meeting everyone. Instead, in a large group, I find a person or two who I can spend time with and talk one on one. I realize how much more meaningful that is to me, and I need to accept that about myself.

I want to accept myself as Christ accepts me. I am introverted, so I must acknowledge that fact. As I take time to learn about myself and spend time with God in His Word, I am encouraged even more by what God says about His love for me and how He has gifted me. When I worship with guitar and song,

I am using my gifts to please God and feeling immense joy and satisfaction in doing it. In these moments, I am able to see my gifts and personality through God's loving eyes.

Father, I pray for those reading this; please graciously reveal their gifts and personality traits to them, showing them the unique and special ways they were created to display a part of Your heart, which no one else can display quite like them. May they be lifted up today in Your arms and carried along by the Holy Spirit. Open a path for their lives, where they have room to be fully themselves. Draw them closer to Your heart than they ever imagined. In Jesus' matchless name, amen.

Journal Response

Shout for joy to the LORD, all the earth. Worship the Lord with gladness; come before him with joyful songs. Know that the Lord is God. It is he who made us and we are his; we are his people, the sheep of his pasture.

PSALM 100:1-3

Each person has unique qualities. Perhaps you're funny or patient or good with cars. What abilities and talents do you possess? How can you use those attributes to serve the Lord and others?

_____

_____

_____

_____

_____

_____

_____

_____

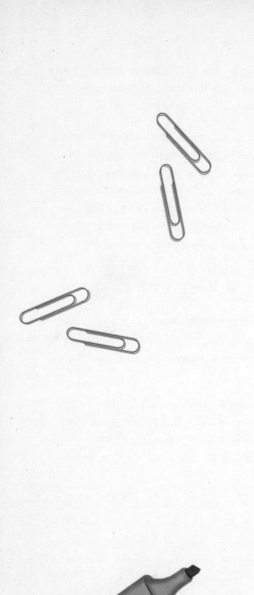

Part 5

Voices of Love and Friendship

*Love never gives up. Love cares more for
others than for self. Love doesn't want what it doesn't have.
Love doesn't strut, doesn't have a swelled head,
Doesn't force itself on others, isn't always "me first,"
Doesn't fly off the handle, doesn't keep score of the sins of others,
Doesn't revel when others grovel,
Takes pleasure in the flowering of truth.*

1 CORINTHIANS 13:4-6, *THE MESSAGE*

*When I have learnt to love God better than my earthly dearest,
I shall love my earthly dearest better than I do now.*

C. S. LEWIS

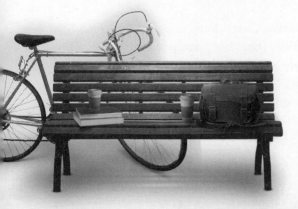

Love Without Getting Tired

By Nicole Chin, Azusa Pacific University

Finally, all of you, live in harmony with one another; be sympathetic, love as brothers, be compassionate and humble. Do not repay evil with evil or insult with insult, but with blessing, because to this you were called so that you may inherit a blessing.

1 PETER 3:8-9

My best friend is anorexic.

I've seen a lot of people abandon her, talk about her behind her back and give her awkward glances when she passes up a hamburger for a salad. But she is my best friend. My. Best. Friend.

She has been struggling with an eating disorder for almost two years now. At first it shocked everyone. I could feel the eyes on us when we walked into the room and hear the whispers and the questions. "She's too thin." "Is she okay?" "Does she have an eating disorder?"

It hasn't been easy. It's been a long, hard road. I've witnessed how some of her friends treat her. Too caught up in their own worlds to really care for her, they throw her aside like it's her problem and she's got to deal with it.

I've been angry and hurt. I've been exhausted and depressed. I've resented her. I've resented myself. And, in the end, the hardest part was being a friend when no one else would. I've discovered selflessness and sacrifice. I've learned how to really love someone. I've realized what true love looks like in its truest, rarest, purest form.

It's love when you spend time with her because everyone else is avoiding her. It's holding her when she won't let anyone near. It's driving her to the doctor's office and waiting an hour in the car. It's eating with her because no one else will. It's confronting and caring for her. It's knowing that you can't fix her, but you can help her. It's love when, despite what she is going through, she's still your best friend, and you will not abandon her.

It's the same love Jesus had for us when He let them nail His wrists to that cross, and the same love that led God to send His Son to earth to face certain death. Amazing love that stretches continents, goes beyond boundaries and finds those crevices in our hearts we hide from most people. Mother Teresa said, "Do not think that love, in order to be genuine, has to be extraordinary. What we need is to love without getting tired."

Journal Response

[Love] believes all things, hopes all things, endures all things.
1 CORINTHIANS 13:7, *NASB*

What qualities in other people make them easy for you to love? What things about you make you more easy or difficult for other people to love? Have you been shown love at your most unlovable times?

_____

_____

_____

_____

33

Grace Revealed

By Erin Harris, Biola University

"For I know the plans I have for you," declares the LORD, "plans to prosper you and not to harm you, plans to give you hope and a future."
JEREMIAH 29:11

Jordan and I talked about a lot of things that had nothing to do with anything. The conversations became deeper and, at 17, Jordan Landon, my best friend in high school, made the first big mistake of her life. She decided to *talk*, to *trust*, to *feel*. She even started sharing her deeper thoughts with me regularly. She was breathing for the first time in her life. But it could not last.

Someone else, a boy in whom she also placed trust, betrayed her secrets. Soon, Jordan's most private struggles—with depression and thoughts of suicide—were public knowledge, and her most intimate thoughts were on display. Having walked her into the deep, the boy left her there to drown. All she could think about was how she would never trust anyone again and how her life had been *fine* until she had opened up. Jordan blamed herself; it was no one's fault but her own.

She sank into deep depression and finally attempted suicide by cutting deep into her wrists. It took the entire year for Jordan to overcome the effects of her emotional degradation. When graduation came in June 2007, it was more than a mere academic victory—it was emotional survival.

I had never felt so incapable of helping someone as I did that year. But I realized that my own experience had prepared me for the part I was called to play in her recovery. During my junior and senior years of high school, I, too, could not get thoughts of suicide out of my head. I wanted it like a needle wants a vein. I steadily took steps in that direction. Although my experience was not as serious as Jordan's, it made me realize what a person is capable of once he or she gives up. I did what I could to help—I listened and prayed and tried not to judge— but I knew from my own experience that no one but God could reach Jordan once she had mentally given up.

Jordan has risen from the ashes and now thrives. Where her painful past used to haunt her, it now helps her recognize and understand the struggles of others around her. When she meets someone else with emotional wounds, she does not avoid them. She embraces them without hesitation and points to God's love, sharing with them her own pain within their struggle.

Ironically, the things we believe we must avoid to emotionally survive—talking, trusting and feeling—are the very things that enable us not only to survive but also to thrive. Why are these acts of empathy and mutual dependence so very vital? They are God's tools, perfectly handled by Christ, to pare away the pain and reveal the grace, love and strength inside. Once this grace, love and strength are shared, life can be embraced as the gift the Creator meant it to be.

Promise Not to Tell

A gossip betrays a confidence, but a trustworthy man keeps a secret.
PROVERBS 11:13

Being a good friend often means keeping other peoples' secrets and protecting their confidences—but that isn't always possible.

Even psychologists, who are ethically and legally required to keep confidential what they're told in sessions, disclose private information when a dangerous situation arises.

When is it time to stop keeping mum? That can be a tough call. If your friend tells you her father is abusing her or your roommate confesses that he has been experimenting with dangerous drugs, you might begin to worry that keeping the secret isn't necessarily the best policy. The fact that you're worrying about it at all is probably a pretty good sign that you should encourage your friend to seek help.

But in a dangerous situation when your friend isn't willing to seek help, there might come a time for you to intervene. Remember: the greatest commandments are to love God and your neighbor. Would breaking your friend's confidence be more loving than keeping it? Remember, there will be consequences—your friend might never forgive you—but sometimes love means losing a friendship to save a friend.

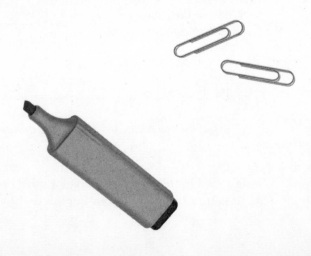

34

The Body of Christ and the Band of the Fighting Irish

By Ricardo Nelson Pineda, Jr., University of Notre Dame

*For just as we have many members in one body and all the members do
not have the same function, so we, who are many, are one body in Christ.*
ROMANS 12:4-5, *NASB*

It was my third and final year in the Notre Dame marching
band—the Band of the Fighting Irish!—and we were heading off
to Penn State for the first time. The plan was to leave early Friday, the day before the game. All 400 band members were to
meet at the band building at 6:30 A.M. sharp. One of the most
important rules in the band is *be on time*.

I made sure everything was ready the night before. My uniform was zipped in its bag and my hat was in its box, ready to go.
I set my alarm for 5:00 in the morning to make sure I'd have
plenty of time to get to the band building.

In retrospect, I remember my alarm ringing, but I turned it
off and lay back down. I woke later to my cell phone ringing.

"Junior, where *are* you?" the voice on the other end asked. It
was my friend Raquel.

"What do you mean?" I looked at the clock. It was 7:15.

"We're on the buses!" Raquel shouted. "We're leaving!"

Panic hit me. My dorm is a good 15-minute walk from the
band building. I begged Raquel to try to stall and hung up the

phone. I threw on my backpack, grabbed my uniform bag and made a run for it. As I sprinted down the hall, my phone rang again. It was Raquel.

"Junior, where are you *now*?"

"Heading downstairs."

"You've got like a minute," she said. "They've already started the buses."

"*A minute?*" I yelled. "Hold them as *long* as you can!"

I burst out the dorm's side door, running. Soon the pain hit. I had just woken up. No breakfast. No stretch. And I had the added weight of my stuffed backpack, uniform bag *and* hatbox. As I neared the library, praying, the phone rang again. I answered it at full gallop, without dropping anything.

"Junior, where are you, buddy?" It was my section leader, Dan.

"Passing by the library," I gasped.

I heard Dan repeat this to someone as I raced around the ROTC building and caught sight of the buses. There were only two left, and both seemed to be moving!

"Dan!" I yelled into the phone. "I can see the buses! Can you see me?"

The front bus braked. Its doors opened and my friend Michael Reeve jumped off. "Give me your stuff!" he yelled running toward me.

I couldn't have been happier as he grabbed my uniform and hatbox, and we both raced toward the bus, stumbling aboard just as the driver took off.

I remember this experience whenever I hear the passage in Romans about the many parts of the Body of Christ. Like a body, the marching band has many members, all of whom play different roles in a great performance. But these members have to learn to work together to overcome obstacles and maintain their unity. They have to rely on each other and look out for each other. I would not have made it to Penn State that day if it were not for Raquel, Dan and Reeve. God bless them. Go Irish!

Journal Response

We have different gifts, according to the grace given us. If a man's gift is prophesying, let him use it in proportion to his faith. If it is serving, let him serve; if it is teaching, let him teach; if it is encouraging, let him encourage; if it is contributing to the needs of others, let him give generously; if it is leadership, let him govern diligently; if it is showing mercy, let him do it cheerfully.

ROMANS 12:6-8

All of us have different personalities, likes and dislikes and abilities. What things do you love to do? What are you good at? What ways do you learn best? What kind of friend are you? How can you use these differences to best serve God and your brothers and sisters in Christ?

_____

_____

_____

_____

_____

_____

_____

_____

35

Searching for a Friend

By Lisa Louie, Azusa Pacific University

The LORD does not look at the things man looks at. Man looks at the
outward appearance, but the LORD looks at the heart.

1 SAMUEL 16:7

In high school, my best friend, Stacy, and I were very much alike. Neither of us wore makeup. We preferred jazz to any other form of music, always did our homework on time, and attended seminars put on for the local senior citizens on "How to Eat Smart." (We also never had boyfriends, but that is beside the point.)

After our senior year, we chose different colleges, and for the first time since the age of two, we found ourselves separated. This went well for a few months while the excitement of our independence was still fresh, but we eventually needed to make other friends. So I began my search, looking for friends as if they had nutrition labels taped to their backs. I would turn them over and look carefully for the exact combination of friendship ingredients I needed.

The trouble was, I couldn't find a single "Stacy." In all my searching, no one came close to my ideal friend. My roommate, Sarah, was an artist like me, but she drew things like dragons and enchanted castles. Next to my watercolor paintings of lilies and Oregon scenery, we seemed like complete opposites. She listened to Fall Out Boy. I listened to Diana Krall. She only wore jeans. I only wore dresses. She was a night person. I was a morning person. The list of opposites was endless.

The first semester of my college career turned out to be one of the loneliest and most challenging times of my life. Luckily, God had something better planned for me the next semester. I didn't give in and change who I was to make friends. I just learned to become sincerely interested in people who weren't just like me. I started asking what Sarah's art pieces meant to her. Soon I wanted to know how many siblings she had and who her third-grade crush was. Whatever I asked her, she would tell me. It's amazing how much I learned. For example, Sarah loves to eat peanut butter right out of the jar. She is freakishly flexible, has one of the most extensive vocabularies of anyone I've ever met, and recently asked me to be a bridesmaid in her upcoming wedding. (Lucky for her, I wear dresses.)

I am not claiming that every seemingly hopeless relationship can magically "click." I know God had a powerful hand in helping me see through my initial selfishness and leading me to find true and loving friends. All He required from me was that I cared enough to seek the beauty in others that He already sees.

Silver and Gold

Make new friends but keep the old;
One is silver and the other gold.

After high school it's easy to lose touch with good friends who head off to schools and other opportunities around the country. Sure, email and Facebook make it pretty easy to keep in touch, but nothing duplicates the experience of opening your campus mailbox and finding something sent by a dear and distant friend.

Here are some ideas to keep in touch:

> *Invest in some good stationery.* Those plain white envelopes and laser-printed letters are as bland and uninviting as porridge. Dress it up a little. How about some heavy blue stationery and a lavender fountain pen?

> *Find an envelope template.* Lots of stationery stores sell them. They're plastic shapes that allow you to create your own envelopes out of magazine covers, old newspapers, sheet music, dust jackets from old books or anything else made of paper.

> *Start a friendship journal.* Find a nice blank journal and send it back and forth through the mail. Send messages, write poems, draw pictures—do anything you want—but just make sure it keeps going back and forth!

36

Not My Will?

By Laurie K. Hekman, Cornerstone University

Your kingdom come, your will be done on earth as it is in heaven.
MATTHEW 6:10

I am facing one of the biggest decisions of my life right now—or so I hear. The decision to get married. I love the man I am dating. I want to marry him, and I want to be with him. But some of the people closest to me have caused us to step back and question our relationship.

We are doing everything "right" according to—and even exceeding—the world's standards. We love God, both of us are a part of a youth ministry, and we have remained as sexually pure as possible, even pledging not to kiss until our wedding day—if that day ever comes.

But some people don't see it. They have this gut sense that something just isn't right.

When I first heard this from some friends, I was outraged. "You are insane!" I told them, in so many words. "How could God tell you and not tell me?"

I had been listening to my own voice in the situation, and I had been figuring that the yes in my heart was a yes from God. Wasn't it?

My missionary friend Tom called me from India a week after this marriage discussion all came out. I told him about what my boyfriend and I were praying about and what he felt for me, but my friend challenged me as well. "Laurie," he said, "have you asked God what He wants for your life yet?"

I stopped. "No," I said, honestly. I hadn't outright asked Him.

Tom moaned. "Oh, Laurie, you've got to do that."

But hadn't I been asking? I had been praying, "God, please show us," and then listening to my own heart—my own will. My will said that it was good—and we weren't sinning, so wasn't it good?

I decided to stop and really ask God. "Father, what do you think?" Almost immediately, I knew the answer, and it was different from the one that I was clinging to in my heart. Could that be Jesus?

Tom told me to read Matthew 6 that night. I thought God would lead me to the "do not worry" verses in that chapter, which would provide comfort. Instead, the Lord's Prayer stood out to me. "Your kingdom come, your will be done." His will.

God's will can be different from mine. I don't like that. Like Jesus in Gethsemane (but on a much, much smaller scale), I am pleading for Him to take a potential cup of pain away from me. "Please, Jesus, can't you just change Your mind?"

In the end, I know that I have to be willing to say, "Not my will, Lord, but Yours."

Journal Response

Therefore do not worry about tomorrow, for tomorrow will worry about itself. Each day has enough trouble of its own.

MATTHEW 6:34

With all our day planners and tight school schedules, it can be easy to seize tight control of our lives rather than follow God's leading and leave the future in His hands. What dreams do you have for the future? Which of those dreams would be difficult to give over to God if He has different plans for you?

_____

_____

_____

_____

_____

_____

_____

_____

_____

_____

_____

_____

_____

_____

_____

_____

_____

Learning How to Love the Abused

By Rachel Watson, Cornerstone University

*If anyone has material possessions and sees his brother in need
but has no pity on him, how can the love of God be in him? Dear children,
let us not love with words or tongue, but with actions and in truth.*
1 JOHN 3:17-18

Tiffany, a humble woman in my dorm, swallowed her fears one night and shared with our discipleship group about the years of abuse she suffered at the hands of her father, mother and step-father. She was beaten, screamed at and belittled, every day. At one point, she witnessed her father raping her mother. He then came into her room and held a gun to her head, threatening to kill her if she breathed a word to anyone.

Even after her aunt and uncle rescued her and adopted her as their own daughter, she feared hugs and kisses. She could not eke out the words "I love you," even to them.

But her aunt never gave up on her. She would chase Tiffany around the house until she trapped her in a hug, and then she would take the child's face in her hands, look into her eyes and say, "I love you, Tiffany, I love you," over and over again.

It might have been easier for her aunt to just let Tiffany shrink away and wrap herself in timid silence. But Tiffany said that what her aunt did was what she needed most. She needed a love that would not let her go.

When I heard her story, I was cut to the core. I realized just exactly how *unloving* I had been all semester to my roommate, who had also been abused by her parents all her life. I knew her story, but I did not know how to talk about it. So I didn't ask. But I should have.

Later, I thanked Tiffany for sharing her story. She told me that my roommate's abuse could explain a lot about why she reacts the way she does to certain things. She encouraged me not to give up, because an abuse victim has only known one way to live and it can take time to heal and change. A victim needs someone to care enough to find out more about her and do things that will build trust.

> *Father, forgive me for my unwillingness to love my roommate unconditionally. Please calm my fears about how she might react if I reach out and bring me new opportunities to mirror Your love to others. Amen.*

Unconditional

It might seem hard to fathom, but the victims of childhood abuse—especially of emotional abuse and neglect—can sometimes have a difficult time recognizing they're victims. If they've been routinely abused at home for years, they might just think that's how normal families operate. After all, what else do they have to compare it to? Many abuse victims also assume they've brought the abuse on themselves by failing to live up to someone else's expectations. They think they're being treated that way because they deserve it. After all, aren't we always told to trust in and rely on grown-ups?

Many victims of abuse are scared, confused, embarrassed and distrustful—even long after they're free of the abusive environment. Remember: the most fundamental and formative relationships in our early lives are with our families—and if that relationship is toxic, it's probably going to affect all our other relationships for a long time.

So be patient. Someone who's been abused has missed out on the stability and unconditional love a family is supposed to offer. It's hard for them to trust others and attach to them. So the best thing for you to do is to just be there. Try to show them the unconditional and constant love of Jesus, and give them time to learn to trust.

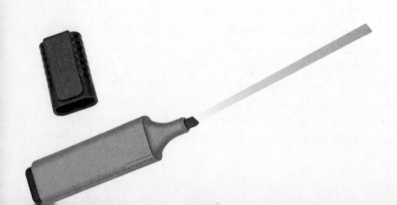

Choosing God

By Jessica Mollo, University of Southern California

But it is good for me to draw near to God:
I have put my trust in the Lord God.
PSALM 73:28, *KJV*

Every "good girl," at one time or another, desires the "bad boy." There is something dangerous, liberating and, of course, *exciting* about dating a guy who does not always follow the rules. In my sophomore year of college, I indulged in this brand of clichéd relationship when I began dating my own bad boy. And, yes, he was the poster child for rebellion: He rode a motorcycle, drank, smoked and engaged in a few "unsavory" activities—to employ a blatant euphemism. Was I trying to fulfill some modern-day James Dean fantasy by dating a "rebel"? Perhaps. But as I look back, I can only utter the words: *What was I thinking?!*

This unhealthy relationship really tested me. I began to make excuses for my boyfriend's behavior, telling myself, *He's trying. He's got a good heart. He wants to be better for me.* That was my first mistake—believing he could change for someone else before he could change for himself.

But I trudged onward, trying to expose him to more enriching experiences. I took him to museums, showed him a few of my favorite classic films and discussed some of my beliefs with him in hopes that he could transition into the good boy.

Then it dawned on me: If I was trying to turn a bad boy into a good one, didn't that mean I just wanted a good boy?

I decided to end the relationship the moment I realized something else: I was drifting farther from God. By spending time with this person, I was denying my religious beliefs and the commitments I had made to God. So I decided to *choose God*.

I understood then that my relationship with the Lord comes before all others. I continually tell myself, *People fail you. Remember that any time you want to put people before God. Love and be loved, but remember that God comes first.* I am learning to honor my promises to God and not neglect Him for any person—no matter how *exciting* that person may seem.

In view of all this, make every effort to respond to God's promises.
Supplement your faith with a generous provision of moral excellence, and
moral excellence with knowledge, and knowledge with self-control, and
self-control with patient endurance, and patient endurance with godliness.

2 PETER 1:5-6, *NLT*

Fixer-upper

For a lot of us, the first house we own will be a fixer-upper—one of those places that's been rented out a few years and perhaps the owners have let fall perilously close to ruin. It needs a new roof, the lawn is dead, and—man!—does it need to be painted. It's nowhere near perfect, but it's what we can afford, and we're willing to put in the hard work to make it something approximating our dream home.

How often do we approach the opposite sex the same way? No relationship is perfect, but how smart is it to enter a relationship with the plan of fully renovating the other person? How fair is it to treat a person like property by designing changes for everything from the individual's wardrobe and hairstyle to his or her diet and hobbies?

Marriage requires lots of adjustments and compromises—both people change as a result of the relationship—and that's a lot of hard work. But, in the same way that you wouldn't buy a house no matter how good it looked if it wasn't structurally sound, there are certain things that go beyond a coat of paint or a reseeded lawn. It's important to prayerfully allow God to show you what He expects in a godly relationship and the kind of person He wants you to be with. If you and your spouse start out headed in different directions, how can you be sure you won't be led off course?

Mommy and Me

By Jessica Schwarzberg, Biola University

*Through love and faithfulness sin is atoned for; through the fear of the
LORD a man avoids evil. . . . In his heart a man plans his course,
but the LORD determines his steps.*

PROVERBS 16:6,9

I walked out of my house determined to show no emotion while
my mother yelled from our doorway. As my car turned the corner, my frozen expression melted and I began to cry. Later, I arrived home to discover all my belongings shoved in trash bags
and piled on our driveway. The knot in my stomach doubled in
size. I recalled the scornful words Mom said to me that morning
and the insulting words *I* said to her. My eyes filled with tears as
I realized that passionate arguments were the extent of our
mother-daughter relationship.

It was the summer after my senior year, and sometime between finals and graduation rehearsal, I decided to accept my
boyfriend's marriage proposal. He had joined the army three
months earlier and had begun intensive training for the war in
Iraq. We declared our never-ending love for one another and decided that marriage was the next step.

Getting married after high school isn't that common, but
what was even stranger was that my parents had no idea of my
plans. I had kept this area of my life, like all other areas, a secret,
and I daily planned my escape. I would pack up my car with

everything it could hold, and—without saying goodbye—I'd drive to Fort Polk, Louisiana.

My plan seemed perfect; but before all the details were arranged, my parents received a call from my boyfriend's grandfather who told them of our plan to elope. My parents were horrified. They sat me down at our kitchen table and flung their insults and condescending opinions at me. But my plans felt right, and I believed that my love for my boyfriend would conquer all things—even my parents' disapproval.

So that day, I stood on my driveway, surrounded by trash bags, and had to decide between my parents and my boyfriend. During the morning's argument, I was given the ultimatum: take your stuff and leave or stay home and forget eloping. I struggled to pick up the stuffed garbage bag and walked toward the front door of my house. I was choosing my family.

When I was 18 and in love, I thought I knew best, and I became hardened to advice. But despite my stubbornness, God showed me that my mom had wise, constructive counsel—and I should listen to it. If I *had* listened to her, and not my own feelings, I could have skipped a lot of pain.

That night, I chose my family because that was the safe decision. But what I later learned was that it was the right decision. After telling my boyfriend I wanted to stay with my family and work on my relationship with my parents before I moved forward in my relationship with him, he broke up with me and got married to someone else three weeks later. He did not understand the importance of my family and didn't value my desire for a godly relationship with them. Although at the time I thought I was in love, God showed me, through my parents, that He has a better plan for my life, which includes a husband who loves both me *and* my family.

Journal Response

My son, do not forget my teaching, but keep my commands in your heart,
for they will prolong your life many years and bring you prosperity.
Let love and faithfulness never leave you; bind them around your neck,
write them on the tablet of your heart. Then you will win favor
and a good name in the sight of God and man.

PROVERBS 3:1-4

In the throes of any deep emotion—whether infatuation or loneliness, exhilaration or depression—it can be difficult to see straight, let alone make sound and prudent decisions. How many angry job resignations are later regretted? How many lovesick tattoos are later removed? In an hour of stability, it might be a good idea to take a personal inventory.

Which emotions are most able to affect your ability to make godly and wise decisions? How can you best prepare now for when those turbulent moments arrive? Who can you most trust to level with you and give you sound advice?

Listen

By Abraham Sherman, Biola University

This is what we speak, not in words taught us by human wisdom but in words taught by the Spirit, expressing spiritual truths in spiritual words.

1 CORINTHIANS 2:13

I've been hearing voices. They have a lot of opinions about my life: "You should ask that other girl out; it doesn't matter that she has different beliefs." "You should be doing more ministry. Hmm, you're not a very good Christian, are you?" "Why are you still going to this school? Your classmates and teachers don't want to hear what you have to say."

Some of the voices are less devious but still raise an eyebrow: "You were right to drop out of that class; you deserve to take it easy." "You're a film major; you need to see as many movies as possible—as research." "What are you worried about? Flirting doesn't hurt anybody."

Then there's one other voice—strong, assured, peaceful and full of authority: "You've trusted Me before in this. Will you again?" "I led you here. I will give you the strength to continue." "Your eyes are on a lesser thing. Only I am worthy of your hope."

Each of these voices has recently grown louder as I've been pursuing a young lady, one who is a faithful servant of the Lord. Nothing scrambles my spiritual sense of direction faster than being interested in someone. Yet few things provide me with an equal opportunity to trust God in the midst of uncertainty, self-condemnation and emotional swings.

In the clearest moments, I hear God telling me to trust His ability to bring me closer to marriage. He encourages me to stick to the plan of getting to know her and being myself around her. He counters my low self-esteem and reassures me that I have something to offer her.

I could never properly pursue a girl without constantly praying and trusting God. I must choose to tune my mind to His voice, which resonates with truth and the fullness of His loving character.

The Holy Spirit has a certain brand of soul He seeks to cultivate in us. His voice plants seeds of love, joy, peace, patience, kindness, goodness, faithfulness, gentleness and self-control (see Galatians 5:22). He speaks of making the Lord our refuge, and of loving His name (see Psalm 5:11).

Reading His Word is daily food and water for our souls. The Word will produce in us, and draw out of us, the substances of direction, trust, courage and continual, dependent prayer. Metabolizing the Word will infuse our prayers with truth and help us recognize His voice. But first we must care to listen.

Journal Response

My sheep listen to my voice; I know them, and they follow me.
I give them eternal life, and they shall never perish.

JOHN 10:27-28

Sometimes God's voice is clear—it's hard to miss that burning bush!—but God's voice comes to us not just in the Bible and in the wise counsel of godly parents and friends. When, in the past, did God speak to you through channels or circumstances that were easy to miss at the time? How might you be more attentive in the future to God's many ways of leading you?

_____
_____
_____
_____
_____
_____
_____
_____
_____
_____
_____
_____
_____
_____
_____
_____

Part 6

Voices of Suffering
and Hope

*We have heard of your faith in Christ Jesus and of the love
you have for all the saints—the faith and love that spring from the hope
that is stored up for you in heaven and that you have already heard
about in the word of truth, the gospel that has come to you.*

<small>COLOSSIANS 1:4-6</small>

*Hope is the thing with feathers that perches in the soul,
And sings the tune without the words, and never stops at all.*

<small>EMILY DICKINSON</small>

*Man can live about forty days without food, about three days without water,
about eight minutes without air . . . but only for one second without hope.*

<small>HAL LINDSEY</small>

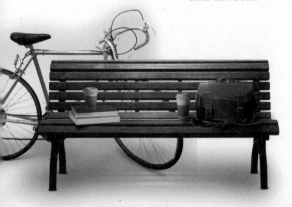

Open Heart Surgery

By Katy Beers, Biola University

So do not fear, for I am with you; do not be dismayed,
for I am your God. I will strengthen you and help you;
I will uphold you with my righteous right hand.

ISAIAH 41:10

On November 18, 1999, I entered Rush Hospital for open heart surgery to repair a one-and-a-half-inch hole in my heart. I was 12 years old. I remember trying hard to act like it wasn't a big deal, but I feared I wouldn't come out of surgery alive.

Once I was under anesthesia, the doctors cut my chest open, sawed my ribs apart, cooled my body temperature to 50 degrees and then stopped my heart for about two hours. They sewed up the hole in my heart muscle and closed my chest back up.

Although it sounds like an extremely painful surgery, what I will never forget was the recovery. I can't adequately describe the agony I endured during the next few months. Not only was I embarrassed about having a five-inch scar down the middle of my chest, but also the pain following the surgery was excruciating. I needed help doing everything: sitting up, eating and even going to the bathroom.

Two months after the surgery, I remember lying in my bed reading my Bible when I came across a verse that caught my attention: "My health may fail, my spirit may grow weak, but God remains the strength of my heart; he is mine forever" (Psalm 73:26, *NLT*). That verse opened my eyes to the fact that no matter what health problem I may encounter or what operations I may suffer through, God will always be with me. He sees and takes note of every second of pain I suffer, and He will not leave me alone when I need Him most.

Pain and Promise

Where can I go from your Spirit? Where can I flee from your presence? If I go up to the heavens, you are there; if I make my bed in the depths, you are there. If I rise on the wings of the dawn, if I settle on the far side of the sea, even there your hand will guide me, your right hand will hold me fast.

PSALM 139:7-10

Sometimes what's best for us hurts a lot, and we can't really judge an event by the amount of pain it produces. It's one thing to get cut by a knife in a dark alley and another thing entirely to get cut open by a skilled surgeon. They both hurt and they both take a long time to heal, but in the case of surgery, the pain only exists to bring about a greater healing.

Pain—mental, emotional and physical—is unpleasant, and we do everything we can to avoid it, but we know that God promises to be with us through our pain and that everything He allows to happen has a purpose. It was, after all, through great pain—a greater pain than any of us will be called upon to endure—that we were redeemed. And it is sometimes through pain that God continues His perfect work in us.

Moving On

By Becky Compton, Azusa Pacific University

*Jesus answered, "If you want to be perfect, go,
sell your possessions and give to the poor, and you will have
treasure in heaven. Then come, follow me."*

MATTHEW 19:21

During the 2007 fall semester, my thoughts were consumed with my parents' divorce and the loss of my family house. (I lived off campus with my parents.) Amazingly, only two days after I moved to a new place, I was assigned to read "Upon the Burning of Our House" by the Puritan poet Anne Bradstreet. I identified with Bradstreet's sense of loss for her house and its memories.

Moving was hard for me—not hard physically, but mentally and emotionally. How do you do homework while moving mid-semester? I had so many plans, but my parents' divorce changed everything. I knew I wouldn't always live in that house, of course. After college, when I had a real job, a friend and I would rent an apartment. Yet I always expected my family home would remain. I had planned to get married in my huge backyard. I had dreamed of putting on my wedding gown in my bedroom (the very room I came home to as a newborn from the hospital). My extra-large dresser, a perfect place for putting on makeup, would stand in its usual spot. Then I would gaze out my back window as the wedding guests arrived.

That long-dreamed-of wedding will not take place at my old address. The announcement of divorce came in the spring of 2006; so, after 16 months, change had to happen. I had to get used to the idea of not living with both parents.

Now I live only with my mom. Although I do something with my dad every Friday and talk to him daily, I still struggle with his absence. When I have some kind of problem at school or need my dad's advice on boys, I can't just walk into his room. Sure, I could go see him whenever I want, but it would be inconvenient to drive the 12 miles to his place when I have homework to do.

Though the spring semester has passed, I am still not used to my new house. However, God knows what to do more than I do. I pray I will be able to help someone who has problems like mine because of what it says in 2 Corinthians 1:3-4: "Praise be to God . . . who comforts us in all our troubles, so that we can comfort those in any trouble with the comfort we ourselves have received from God." God reminded me of this comfort two days after I moved, when I read Bradstreet's "Upon the Burning of Our House," which talks about putting your hope in heaven instead of earthly treasures.

> *Thou hast an house on high erect*
> *Fram'd by that mighty Architect,*
> *With glory richly furnished,*
> *Stands permanent tho' this bee fled.*
> *It's purchased, and paid for too*
> *By him who hath enough to doe.*
> ANNE BRADSTREET

Journal Response

Do not store up for yourselves treasures on earth,
where moth and rust destroy, and where thieves break in and steal.
But store up for yourselves treasures in heaven, where moth and rust
do not destroy, and where thieves do not break in and steal.
For where your treasure is, there your heart will be also.
MATTHEW 6:19-21

We can't resist the question—it's like the ones
about what books you'd take to a desert island,
or the historical people you'd invite to dinner:
If your house were burning down and you could
only save three possessions, what would they be?
Really think about it before you answer. Did you
tend to favor things of monetary or sentimental
value? What does your answer reveal about
the intangible things you value most?

Releasing the Reins

By Renae Matz, Union University

He reached down from on high and took hold of me;
he drew me out of deep waters.
2 SAMUEL 22:17

I surrender all. I surrender all.
All to Thee, my Blessed Savior,
I surrender all.
JUDSON W. VAN DEVENTER

I have spent hours of my life absentmindedly singing the lyrics to this catchy invitational song, without thinking about the profound statement it makes. Surrendering to the Lord isn't a simple statement we can repeat. It's a feeling of desperation that radiates from the innermost part of our being. It's the place we reach at rock bottom when we realize there is absolutely nothing else we can do. In this place, we're powerless. It's as though life zooms by but we stand perfectly still, incapable of moving. Even if we were to move, it would be pointless, because we would have no impact on the outcome.

It's the place I found myself after an F4 tornado ripped through my home at Union University. For those of us who were on campus, we will forever have the sights, smells and emotions engraved on our hearts and our memories.

For me, I reached the place of total surrender about an hour after the tornado touched down. We were huddled in classrooms waiting for another storm cell to come. After sitting in there for about five minutes, one of my roommates experienced an asthma attack, which quickly turned into a panic attack that gripped her entire body. We tried our best to calm her, but it was to no avail. I felt frustrated because we were totally powerless. We could do nothing but watch our friend suffer. I remember muttering, "Oh, Lord, no. Please, Lord, no," over and over. It was my repeated plea to God, and all I could express.

In that short, repeated plea, I was giving my friend up to God. There was nothing I could do. Surrendering doesn't come easy for me. But since that night, in so many different ways, I have learned that God is always with me. He already has all the power and control in His hands. My own sense of power is an illusion. I can do nothing. I am nothing. But God is everything.

Ever feel stressed? Just surrender. I say that as if it were easy. It's not. It's a deliberate act of trusting God. When you reach the place of total dead ends and all you can do is seek God's face and plead for mercy, He's quick to answer. He's always with us. God is the Door in the Hallway of Dead Ends. And He's calling for us—a call to surrender.

Journal Response

*A furious squall came up, and the waves broke over the boat, so that it
was nearly swamped. Jesus was in the stern, sleeping on a cushion.
The disciples woke him and said to him, "Teacher, don't you care if we
drown?" He got up, rebuked the wind and said to the waves, "Quiet!
Be still!" Then the wind died down and it was completely calm. He said
to his disciples, "Why are you so afraid? Do you still have no faith?"*

MARK 4:37-40

There's nothing that brings us to our knees
like a cataclysmic natural event. Hurricanes,
earthquakes and tornadoes remind us of how small
we are and how big God's world really is. How can
we keep mindful of this sense of scale during the
smaller storms that brew up in our lives? How can
we keep surrendering to God, even when it looks like
we can handle the situation on our own?

He Never Leaves . . .

By Karla Florence Noles, New Orleans Baptist Theological Seminary

For the Lord will not reject [us] forever. Even if He causes suffering,
He will show compassion according to His abundant faithful love.
LAMENTATIONS 3:31-32, *HCSB*

It was a rainy Saturday morning in mid April, and I knew it was back. I had cried all night long, and that morning, I was in the library writing in my journal, its pages blotted with teardrops. I didn't know why, but something inside me, affected by a series of emotional and physical stressors, hurt deeply. I had felt this way six years before when I was a freshman in college. Now I was completing my first year at seminary, and I knew the clinical depression had returned.

Being depressed in a Christian environment can be so difficult because *Christians aren't supposed to be depressed*. But as young people who are seeking to follow and obey the desires of our God, we must realize that the enemy will try to ensnare us in any way he can. He wants us to turn away from God and do the things that will somehow dull the pain. He wants us to get angry with our Lord and doubt His goodness to His children. The temptation was there to turn away, but where else could I go?

It was a long and agonizing year before I was completely healed; but God did so much refining and purifying in my life. I questioned God and I wrestled with Him, asking why He would allow such pain. He brought up so many deeply buried sins of unbelief, selfishness and pride—and I was ashamed of myself and ashamed of my weakness. But in my weakness, He proved Himself strong.

If we belong to the Lord, He's going to take us through those valleys. Sometimes the pain can be devastating, but when we look up, we can see and trust that God sees us in our pain. His way is good and right, and though we don't understand it, He is doing something wonderfully glorious that will far exceed anything we could ever have dreamed. He allows the pain, but only so He can show His glory. So let's allow Him to comfort us in our pain and confusion, because He is indeed close to the brokenhearted.

Disclosing

Taking medication or being treated for depression or some other disorder is nothing to be ashamed of, but letting people know about it can still be difficult. Should you confide in a few close friends or boldly make it known to anyone who might be interested? At what point in a friendship do you make this disclosure?

This is your private life, so it's up to you to decide when and to whom you reveal your situation; but be aware that there are healthy and unhealthy reasons for wanting to do so. Having friends who know about your struggles can offer you a healthy source of support and encouragement, and being open about your situation can offer you a sense of freedom and release. After all, they know this about you, and they still love you, right? But there are also unhealthy reasons for disclosing. Might you be playing for sympathy? Trying to manipulate others into treating you differently? Using your situation as an excuse for things that aren't really caused by it?

Focus

By Jonathan Blake, California State University, Fullerton

Be joyful always; pray continually; give thanks in all circumstances,
for this is God's will for you in Christ Jesus.
1 THESSALONIANS 5:16-18

I'm not much of a golfer, but I appreciate the game of golf as a metaphor. I was out playing with my dad, and the first hole featured a sand trap. I asked my dad for advice on what club to use to avoid the trap, and he told me, "Jon, there is no sand trap."

Profound!

Now, what my dad probably meant was, "You call *that* a sand trap?" But what I heard was something much deeper and more sublime: that I should not think of the sand as a trap but rather as part of the course. If I go in, I go in. What's the worst that could happen? I add a few strokes to my score? I don't mean to speak golf heresy, but wouldn't it be better if every aspect of the course were appreciated?

Might not God intend us to learn something while we're in the sand? I think of Joseph in the dungeon; I think of Paul and Silas in prison; I think of those ten-and-a-half months I spent working at McDonalds. Sure, it was terribly unpleasant, but the experience contributed to who I am today. And even with that, Paul didn't write, "Find something good about the situation, and give thanks." He wrote, "Give thanks in all circumstances, for this is God's will for you in Christ Jesus." If Job can say, "Though he slay me, yet will I hope in him" (Job 13:15), I think I can make it through a few sand traps.

It's easy to get caught up in the idea that if something good happens I should be happy, or that if something bad happens I should be sad. But I feel that if I practice giving thanks in all circumstances, I will begin to see them simply as circumstances and not label them *good* or *bad*.

Sand is sand; it is we who make it a trap.

Rejoice!

"Rejoice in the Lord always" (Philippians 4:4). Sounds easy, doesn't it? We all know it isn't, and the apostle Paul, who wrote this verse, knew it better than any of us. In 2 Corinthians 11:24-27, he offers us a small catalogue of what his life was like:

Five times I received from the Jews the forty lashes minus one. Three times I was beaten with rods, once I was stoned, three times I was shipwrecked, I spent a night and a day in the open sea, I have been constantly on the move. I have been in danger from rivers, in danger from bandits, in danger from my own countrymen, in danger from Gentiles; in danger in the city, in danger in the country, in danger at sea; and in danger from false brothers. I have labored and toiled and have often gone without sleep; I have known hunger and thirst and have often gone without food; I have been cold and naked.

None of us will likely face anything close to what Paul faced—*three* shipwrecks!—so how much more reason do we have to keep rejoicing!

Peace That Passes Understanding

By Cathy Hansen, Azusa Pacific University

Praise our God, O peoples, let the sound of his praise be heard;
he has preserved our lives and kept our feet from slipping. For you, O God,
tested us; you refined us like silver . . . we went through fire and water,
but you brought us to a place of abundance.

PSALM 66:8-10,12

I discovered that the big Bible in the prayer chapel was opened to Psalm 66 when I wandered in a few nights ago. I was walking across campus, toward home, and felt a desire to visit the chapel. I followed the instinct only to find that I was following the Spirit.

Life had been rough lately. I loved my major, but I felt swamped with the constant reading and writing that stole from both my social time and sleep. My grandma was diagnosed with lung cancer, and—just like that—it was at stage four. It had spread to her brain and spine and bones. Furthermore, I'd spent more than a year in a relationship with a guy who wouldn't commit to calling it a relationship. The pain of finally letting him go, and of writing off all the time and hope I'd invested in him, hurt like nothing I'd gone through before.

I felt overwhelmed. I took a walk around campus, desperately asking God where He would lead me next, because I didn't know what to do anymore. I finally gave up and began my walk home—right past the prayer chapel, where God was waiting patiently to give me Psalm 66.

I could do nothing but stare at the verses as I was impressed by their truth. Yes, things had been rough in my life and I was feeling overwhelmed, but had God ever let my feet slip? On the contrary, He had always been faithful to me. I had finally reached a place of earnestly seeking Him; before, I had been too selfish and full of pride to give my burdens completely to Him.

"If I had cherished sin in my heart," the psalm reads in verses 18 and 19, "the Lord would not have listened; but God has surely listened and heard my voice in prayer." Once I took the small step of confessing that I could not control my own life, God broke through the walls of sin, took control and healed my pain.

It has not been an instant fix—I still have to deal with all of life's problems—however, it has opened the door for God to share with me His peace that surpasses all understanding, while together we work out my life.

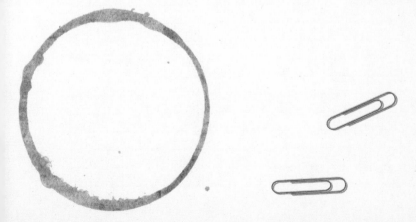

Journal Response

Ask and it will be given to you; seek and you will find;
knock and the door will be opened to you. For everyone who
asks receives; he who seeks finds; and to him who
knocks, the door will be opened.

MATTHEW 7:7-8

It's the idea we never stop learning: When things
are complicated, and we're torn in a million different
directions by worries, the answer is to keep it
simple. Seek God first (see Matthew 6:25-34).
Why is that so hard to remember? What does it
mean to seek His kingdom and His righteousness?
Looking over the things you have to do this
week, how can you seek God first?

_____

_____

_____

_____

_____

_____

_____

_____

_____

_____

_____

_____

_____

_____

Sufficient Grace

By Allison Jean Hart, Santa Clara University

My grace is sufficient for thee: for my strength is made perfect in weakness.
2 CORINTHIANS 12:9, *KJV*

A typical day for me during winter quarter consisted of early morning crew practice, class until 3:20 P.M., another practice at 4:00 P.M., and then the day would end in a chaotic attempt to finish all my homework due the next day. I would try to be in bed and asleep by midnight, so I could get up to do it all over again—and I was very lucky if this actually happened. As a double major in biology and communication, this was no easy task. I continued to push through, trying to stay strong in the midst of my very busy life.

The harder I pushed through, the more difficult my personal life became. I got in a car crash, which left me with a concussion and bruised ribs. Normally this wouldn't be a big deal, but I was stuck in California with no family for support. Soon after my accident, I got a call that my aunt had committed suicide. Then one of my closest friends was hospitalized due to her eating disorder—and I never even knew her problem had gotten that bad. Past feelings related to my self-image came back, and I started cutting myself again—something I hadn't done in almost a year.

At first, I was furious at God. How could He do this to me? All I was trying to do was love Him, but He would bring up past experiences and pains just to watch me fall yet again. I was tired of being strong. I was sick of people telling me I had the strength to get through it.

After opening my Bible to 2 Corinthians 12:9 one tear-filled night, I realized that I didn't have to be strong at all. In fact, I realized I can be as weak as I need to be—because God finds His strength in that weakness. I am never alone when faced with trying times; God is always there to carry me through.

We may not understand why certain things happen, but there is a purpose behind it all. God has no intention of hurting us. In fact, most of the time we hurt ourselves because we are so caught up in our lives that we forget they aren't even ours to begin with.

In college, I have learned to take a step back, breathe and realize God has it all under control. All I have to do is have faith.

Journal Response

And we know that all things work together for good to them that love God, to them who are the called according to his purpose.

ROMANS 8:28, *KJV*

Think about some catastrophes in your more distant past. What did you learn from those events? How did God strengthen you through them? How should this shed light on the problems you face today?

_____

_____

_____

_____

_____

_____

Relying on God

Author and University Names Withheld

In the same way, the Spirit helps us in our weakness. We do not know what we ought to pray for, but the Spirit himself intercedes for us with groans that words cannot express. And he who searches our hearts knows the mind of the Spirit, because the Spirit intercedes for the saints in accordance with God's will.

ROMANS 8:26-27

The cutting began when I was 11. At first it was something I did occasionally when I felt desperate and needed to release my anger. When I was 12, my dad, who had already divorced my mother, moved to San Francisco. I stayed in Southern California with my sister and my grandfather. At that point, things got worse. I began to cut myself regularly.

I found a strange comfort in knowing I was in control of what I was doing. I found comfort in the predictability. Each time I cut myself would feel exactly the same, and the result would be the same. It was the only part of my life I could depend on. There was no one else I could rely on—not my alcoholic, abusive mother, not my absent father, not my resentful sister.

So I kept cutting, and eventually I began to consider suicide a reasonable solution to my problems; there seemed to be no point living in such a painful and unloving world. I eventually took a handful of mixed pills. I survived that night—having taken mostly ibuprofen and allergy pills—but the suicidal thoughts didn't stop, and life didn't get any easier.

When I was 13, a friend invited me to her youth group. I was reluctant to go, but when I got there, I noticed something different about the kids—they were happy. When it came time for the message, I was surprised to hear how much Jesus loved the people who seemed least lovable. The possibility that there was a God who loved me in spite of everything I had done, and everything I was doing, was unfathomable. The youth pastor gave me my first Bible that night, and I read it eagerly to learn about this mysterious Jesus who healed people, forgave sins and offered unconditional love. I'd like to say I changed overnight, but that's not what happened.

When I was 14, my sister, trying to get me in trouble, told my dad that I had been cutting. My dad threatened to kick me out of the house if I didn't stop. It felt like the absolute worst thing that could possibly have happened: my sister and my dad took away the one thing I relied on, the one thing that was truly mine. No longer able to rely on cutting, I had to learn to rely on God. Stopping was a long, difficult and lonely path, and my relationship with God was the only thing that helped rid me of my addiction.

Through my painful experience with depression and cutting, I learned that God loves me deeply and does not want me to carry my burdens alone. We need to be aware that even Christians sometimes struggle with depression and addictions, but we no longer have to carry our burdens alone. Christ is ready and willing to carry them with us.

Journal Response

In this world you will have trouble. But take heart!
I have overcome the world.
JOHN 16:33

Greater is he that is in you, than he that is in the world.
1 JOHN 4:4, *KJV*

Everyone faces struggles of many sorts. Yet we do not have to face these difficulties alone. God is with us even in painful times. Do you find comfort in knowing God is with you? What keeps you from seeking God when problems come into your life? What thwarts your efforts in believing God is really there to help you?

_____

_____

_____

_____

_____

_____

_____

_____

_____

_____

_____

_____

_____

_____

Part 7

Voices of Humanity and the World

Later Jesus appeared to the Eleven as they were eating; he rebuked them for their lack of faith and their stubborn refusal to believe those who had seen him after he had risen. He said to them, "Go into all the world and preach the good news to all creation."

MARK 16:14-15

You did not choose me, but I chose you and appointed you to go and bear fruit—fruit that will last. Then the Father will give you whatever you ask in my name. This is my command: Love each other.

JOHN 15:16-17

Those who love not their fellow beings live unfruitful lives.

PERCY BYSSHE SHELLEY

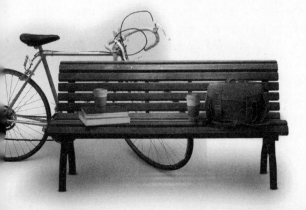

49

Community Dogs and the Least of Our Brothers

By Adrienne Chaudoin, Taylor University

And the King will answer them, "Truly, I say to you, as you did it to one of the least of these my brothers, you did it to me."
MATTHEW 25:40, *ESV*

Walking the streets of Thessaloniki, Greece, on a class trip, I noticed a few dogs running around. Our tour guide informed us that our group was witnessing "community dogs." Community dogs are stray dogs that the people of the city adopt. These dogs live on the streets, and anyone with an extra bit of food throws it to them. Parents take their children to the park and let their kids play with the dogs. Tourists, like me, take pictures with the cute ones.

When our group reached Athens, things were no different. Dogs wandered up to us, taking us for suckers, somehow knowing we were tourists. One portly dog in particular took a liking to us. We named him Fatty and paid him lots of attention. We let him sit at our feet at outdoor cafés and fed him under the table.

One particular evening, I was out late. The streets were almost void of people and dogs. I rounded a corner and stopped in my tracks. There, in the corner between two buildings, were about 15 dogs snuggling with each other amidst the trash.

That's when it struck me: These dogs were no different from the homeless. Where New York City or Chicago had homeless people and rarely a stray dog, Thessaloniki and Athens had homeless dogs with rarely a stray person. Hardest for me to realize was how I was treating these dogs compared to how I treated the poor back home. In New York, I would cross the street to avoid mumbling "sorry" at them, without making eye contact. In Athens, I would call for Fatty to come to me. I would take pictures hugging or petting a stray dog, but I would angle my camera to avoid the homeless person in the background. What is wrong with this picture?

Homeless people and stray dogs: during the day they are found roaming the streets, looking for food or sitting in the park. At night, they're not seen except down an alley with trash and newspapers keeping them warm. At times they huddle together to keep warm.

I gave Fatty food because he was the cutest, and I would give a businessman extra change to use the phone booth because he lost his cell phone. I didn't give the homeless person food, and I didn't give him change when he needed it.

People, even more so than dogs, are a part of our community. It's time we started treating them, whether in need or not, like our brothers and sisters, our fellow human beings loved by Christ.

> *A generous man will himself be blessed,*
> *for he shares his food with the poor.*
> PROVERBS 22:9

Journal Response

*I was hungry and you gave me nothing to eat, I was thirsty
and you gave me nothing to drink, I was a stranger and you did not
invite me in, I needed clothes and you did not clothe me, I was sick
and in prison and you did not look after me.*

MATTHEW 25:42-43

It's easy to turn away from people. We do it so
often and for so many reasons—and not just to the
homeless man on the street who wants to know if
we have change. What are the things we see in other
people that make us instinctively want to turn away?
How would Jesus respond to the same person?

_____

_____

_____

_____

_____

_____

_____

_____

_____

_____

_____

_____

_____

_____

_____

_____

_____

_____

50

The Least of These

By Jamalin Harp, Abilene Christian University

He who oppresses the poor shows contempt for their Maker,
but whoever is kind to the needy honors God.

PROVERBS 14:31

We shuffled our tired bodies through the mass of people, and I reached for one of the long, smooth metal poles. I grasped it and braced for the lurch of the subway car. With tired legs and aching feet, I longed to collapse into one of the seats. It was late in the afternoon; we had been awake since 5:00 A.M. and had trekked up and down the streets of New York City since 8:30. For three college students from Texas, we had done a sufficient job of navigating our way through the city.

Within moments of the subway's departure, he appeared. He personified one of the great New York stereotypes that had rooted in my mind years ago. He was a homeless man.

We had seen several homeless people that day, but most had kept to themselves. This man, however, stood only 10 feet away on the opposite side of the subway car. He was tall, with a large worn jacket and dreadlocked shoulder-length hair. He wore large black-framed glasses. He began talking and telling those around that he was in need of anything we could give him. His eyes searched the crowd and locked with mine; discomfort, guilt and sorrow flooded me all at once. Acting on a developed instinct,

I looked away, pretending not to see him. I surveyed the people around me—a sea of faces offered up the same monotonous, uninvolved look. Some pretended to be immersed in their paperback books or whatever was playing on their iPods. Others stared vacantly into space. Every blank face seemed to scream, "As far as I'm concerned, I'm the only one on this subway."

My mind raced with conflicting thoughts. *It's my duty to help this man, but didn't I hear somewhere that the homeless of New York make somewhere in the neighborhood of $100,000 a year?*

I resolved to give the man some change, but as I reached for my purse, the subway swayed suddenly, forcing me to grab the pole again and hold on tightly until we stopped. The doors opened and we all got off. Later that day, I dropped a few coins in another homeless man's cup—my effort to make reparations for my previous indecisiveness. Yet I couldn't escape the miserable thought that burrowed deep inside me: I had seen someone who was in true need and had neglected to help him. I failed in serving "the least of these."

The One Who Has Food

There are more than 300 verses in the Bible that talk about the poor and how we should treat them. Jesus spoke more about the poor than He did about the rich, but the poor are easy to forget and easy to avoid. Many college campuses, both Christian and secular, have student-run social justice ministries that reach out to the homeless and the poor, and it's easy to get involved. But even if no such program exists, why not skip a meal in the cafeteria with some friends, request the brown bag lunch instead and go out and find someone who can use it?

51

A House for Faith

By Christina Waken, California State University, Long Beach

Then the word of the LORD came through the prophet Haggai:
"Is it a time for you yourselves to be living in your paneled houses,
while this house remains a ruin?"
HAGGAI 1:3-4

The hot Louisiana sun beat down relentlessly on my tired arms as I pounded a final nail into the roof before heading home. While my friends were lounging by the beach back home, I had spent my spring break driving nails and sawing wood in the bayous of New Orleans as part of a team of student volunteers. I climbed down the ladder and surveyed our work. The skeleton of beams that had greeted us when we arrived the week before was slowly taking the shape of a house, but the work was far from done.

The vicious winds and subsequent floods generated by Hurricane Katrina several years before had left most of New Orleans a wasteland of empty houses, heaped debris and splintered dreams. Each swing of my hammer was my attempt to piece back together all that had been shattered by the storm. Now the week of construction was over, and my heart sank as I realized that despite days of pouring our sweat and love into each nail and beam, we would have to leave the house unfinished.

Before we left the work site for the last time, our foreman asked us to sign the house for the homeowner, whose name was

Faith. As I searched for a smooth board to write on, I began to read the notes left by other groups that had come before us. Their loving words were everywhere, on every plank and every surface. *Hundreds must have had a hand in this house*, I thought. Suddenly, my restless heart was overwhelmed by an extraordinary peace. I knew that just as God had brought so many builders before me, He would continue to send His servants to complete the project and turn Faith's house into a home.

Katrinas of every kind have left our world, like the streets of New Orleans, in shambles, tearing lives apart and wreaking havoc upon hearts. My week of rebuilding Faith's home made me understand that the love of our heavenly Father alone has the power to resurrect the rubble, but He longs to reveal that love through His people. While love's tools take many forms—like a hammer or a pen—love's hands are our very own. As the Great Workman, God is faithful to mend the broken, but He calls on *us*, His children, to step outside ourselves and offer up our hands in obedience to restore a world in ruins.

And I said, "Here am I. Send me!"
ISAIAH 6:8

If I Had a Hammer

While the hurricane-ravaged Gulf Coast haunted us with countless heartrending images of devastation in the wake of Hurricane Katrina, there are homeless families *everywhere* across the U.S. And if you're willing to swing a hammer, you can help.

Founded in 1976 by Millard and Linda Fuller, and by using volunteer labor, Habitat for Humanity has built more than

250,000 houses around the world, which now house more than 1 million people.

These modest but decent houses are made available, at no profit, to families in need—and the housing payments those families make over the years provide the funds to build more homes.

Hundreds of universities and schools around the U.S. have their own student-run campus chapters of Habitat, and many local churches are also involved, so opportunities to get involved are easy to come by.

Also, Habitat's Collegiate Challenge program offers groups of five or more students the opportunity to spend a week building houses at construction sites across the U.S. Since 1989, more than 100,000 students have participated, usually during spring break. If you'd like to see if your college has its own Habitat chapter, you can do so online at www.habitat.org.

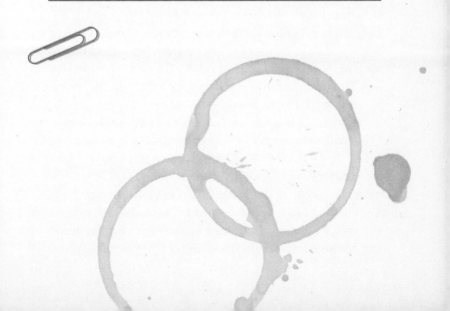

52

Whatever Doesn't Kill You

By Joshua Prichard, San Francisco State University

All that the Father gives Me will come to Me, and whoever comes to Me I will certainly not cast out.
JOHN 6:37, *NASB*

I was heading to my afternoon film history class when I heard the ruckus. A group had gathered out in the quad. People were shouting. Others were holding signs. I headed over to see what the commotion was about. I soon learned that a small, off-campus church group had pulled up in a van. They had walked to the middle of campus holding up signs. The sign closest to me read HOMOSEXUALS WILL BURN IN HELL in big red letters. The group had drawn a crowd, and a shouting match was in full swing. It looked like things could turn ugly very quickly, but I couldn't stay to see what happened. I was late for class.

The next day, the student newspaper printed an article about the incident. They claimed this small church group had harassed students for hours. Afraid the scene might turn violent, campus police had escorted the group from campus. Although I had nothing to do with it, the incident left me sad and disturbed. Everyone on campus had read or heard about what happened, and it wasn't the first time something like this had taken place.

I had come to San Francisco State because it had a film school that was affordable, certified and accommodating to my mediocre academic standing. I had fallen in love with the city a few years earlier, and it was the only school at which I had applied. The biggest dilemma I faced was one I'd encountered before: As a young Christian, I had to be capable of living in a secular world without losing my spiritual values.

This dilemma rang especially true for me. In pursuit of a career in the film business, in a public university and in an extremely left-wing city, I knew it would be a struggle from the get-go. I was enrolled in a school where, as a Christian, I was outnumbered 10 to 1.

When I moved into the dorm, I didn't know anybody, let alone any strong Christians. It didn't take me too long to find out what stereotypes people would project onto me, and that van full of sign-carrying churchgoers didn't help any. I know that homosexuality is a sticky subject for the Church, but the most important lesson Christ taught us was to show compassion to *everyone*. That group of Christians who visited our campus seemed motivated by something other than love and a desire to share the gospel. After they left, I came to realize they embodied a stereotype that I, as a believer in a very secular place, had to try every day to live down.

As a Christian, I came to this most liberal of cities expecting to be challenged—maybe even persecuted and mocked—for what I believed. But I soon realized that the mocking and persecution cut both ways. As a Christian, I came to San Francisco to study filmmaking, thinking that I had a message to share, but I soon humbly realized I had a lot to learn as well: San Francisco is one of the most open and embracing cities in the world. Perhaps the Church could learn something of that, too.

Journal Response

"Teacher, which is the greatest commandment in the Law?" Jesus replied:
" 'Love the Lord your God with all your heart and with all your soul and
with all your mind.' This is the first and greatest commandment. And the
second is like it: 'Love your neighbor as yourself.' All the Law and the
Prophets hang on these two commandments."

MATTHEW 22:36-40

When Jesus tells us how important it is to love
our neighbor, He isn't just talking about people who
share our outlook and beliefs. What does it mean to
act lovingly to those whose lifestyles or beliefs we
might disagree with? How do we show love to those
who might persecute and mock us? Who might we,
as Christians, be tempted to persecute and mock?

_____

_____

_____

_____

_____

_____

_____

_____

_____

_____

_____

_____

_____

_____

53

Race

By Michelle Hopf, Auburn University

Here there is no Greek or Jew, circumcised or uncircumcised, barbarian, Scythian, slave or free, but Christ is all, and is in all.

COLOSSIANS 3:11

One day, I was given the opportunity to help out at an organization called Lifesavers: Saturday Sunday School. The organization sends buses to low-income areas of the community to pick up children ages 3 to 12 and bring them together for a worship service, kid style.

I went to the service for the older half of the children. The music was loud. Kids ran back and forth every which way. The room buzzed with energy. Praise and worship started. Some kids really got into it, singing as loudly as they could and dancing the day away.

When we were settling down for games, the little girl next to me asked a simple question: "Is Jesus white?" She asked as if she already knew the answer. I stumbled over my words as I told her He was of Hebrew descent. He probably looked like the people of the Middle East, where Israel is. I could not get over the sound of hopelessness in her voice. *He wasn't like me.* Who knows what was going through her head? I could have overanalyzed this situation in a big way, but what if I didn't?

Western media has consistently portrayed Jesus as a white man, and just how detrimental that one-dimensional image can be struck me that day. Children notice a lot more details than people give them credit for. As far as race goes, it's like Paul says: "Christ is all, and is in all."

A portrait of Jesus Christ hangs in my church. Standing back you see Christ, but as you move closer to it, you see faces. The faces of many people, of many ethnicities, make up the Body of Christ in the painting. The same statement holds true for people. Christ was indeed a man, but together we all make up the Body of Christ. Color is not relevant. "Christ is all, and is in all."

The Segregated Hour

In a 1963 interview, Dr. Martin Luther King, Jr., was asked whether integration wouldn't likely begin in local churches and spread to the rest of American culture. Dr. King answered, "We must face the fact that in America, the church is still the most segregated major institution in America. At 11:00 on Sunday morning, when we stand and sing that Christ has no east or west, we stand at the most segregated hour in this nation."

More than 30 years later, in 1997, a Gallup Poll confirmed that Dr. King's observation was still largely true in the U.S. While people of different races work together and play together and go to school together, they tend not to worship together. Seventy-three percent of whites worshiped at churches that were mostly or all white, and 71 percent of African-Americans worshiped at churches that were mostly or all African-American.[1]

Note

1. George H. Gallup Jr., "The Most Segregated Hour: Religion and Social Trends," *Gallup, Inc.,* July 9, 2002. http://www.gallup.com/poll/6367/Most-Segregated-Hour.aspx (accessed January 2009).

54

On the Rocks

By Heather Buchanan, Chapman University

" 'Love the Lord your God with all your heart and with all your soul and with all your mind and with all your strength.' The second is this: 'Love your neighbor as yourself.' There is no commandment greater than these."

MARK 12:30-31

"Don't ask me complicated questions right now," my suitemate said. Her voice was slurred and changed pitch randomly.

"I just asked how you were," I replied.

"I am having *so* much fun," she said. There was a dull thud on her end of the line. "Oh. Ha, ha. Sorry. What do you want, Poodle?"

I pulled the receiver away from my ear to avoid her too-loud laughter. "I'm at Disneyland with Heidi," I said. "We wanted directions to that restaurant you told us about." There was a long pause. I pictured her standing in somebody's crowded backyard, trying to scratch her head while holding both her phone and her red plastic cup full of who knows what.

"Um-m-m . . ." Her voice trailed off. I could practically hear her forehead wrinkle.

"Never mind," I said. "We'll figure it out. Bye."

When I returned to the dorm that night, I found her standing in the doorway of the bathroom that separated our rooms. She cocked her head and smiled.

"Hey, Poodle," she tittered. "Where's Mike? I *need* to find Mike."

"What happened?" I asked.

She looked down at her shoes, embarrassed. "I wanted to see if my phone could fit in the bed post," she said. "It does. Now I can't get it out." She perked up suddenly. "I'm going to go do my laundry!" She lurched back into her room and rummaged around in her closet. At three in the morning, I was too tired to care. If she was going to drink, *she'd* have to deal with the consequences. I went to bed without saying goodnight.

The next morning, I poked my head into her room. She lay in a crumpled pile of blankets. Over her pulled-down sheets, she gave me a halfhearted smile.

"How are you feeling?" I asked her, though I already had a pretty good idea. "Have fun last night?"

She moaned. "I don't remember a thing. Somehow my laundry is done and my phone is wedged into the bedpost."

I sat on the edge of her bed, trying not to aggravate her headache. "Luckily, Andrea came over," she said. "She baby-sat me all night and made sure I didn't do anything stupid."

At that moment, I felt an unexpected pang of guilt. Why hadn't *I* been the one to sit up with her to make sure she was okay? As a Christian at a secular school, it's sometimes hard to know when to judge and when to comfort. I know I'm supposed to live a different life from the people around me, but how am I supposed to react to *their* lives?

"That was really nice," I said, feeling suddenly lazy and self-absorbed. Even if I didn't approve of her drinking, I should have been there when she needed me. "Andrea's a good friend."

She closed her eyes, and I put my hand on her knee, as if that gesture might somehow make her feel better. But the gesture, I realized, was really more for me. It was a promise that, as her Christian friend, I would try harder to put compassion before condemnation.

Journal Response

But a Samaritan, as he traveled, came where the man was; and when he saw him, he took pity on him. He went to him and bandaged his wounds, pouring on oil and wine. Then he put the man on his own donkey, took him to an inn and took care of him.

LUKE 10:33-35

God wants us to have compassion for others, but like many of His commandments, compassion isn't always easy. What aspects in others make it difficult to feel compassion for them? How would Jesus treat those people? How might we overcome our failure to be compassionate?

Part 8

Voices of Growth
and Decision

*When Jesus spoke again to the people, he said,
"I am the light of the world. Whoever follows me will never
walk in darkness, but will have the light of life."*

JOHN 8:12

*Let us be of good cheer, remembering that the misfortunes
hardest to bear are those which never happen.*

JAMES RUSSELL LOWELL

*Finish each day and be done with it. . . . You have done what you could;
some blunders and absurdities no doubt crept in; forget them as soon as
you can. Tomorrow is a new day; you shall begin it well and serenely.*

RALPH WALDO EMERSON

55

Adding to the Brightness

By Rebekah Cooper, Biola University

*In the same way, let your light shine before men, that they may
see your good deeds and praise your Father in heaven.*
MATTHEW 5:16

When I stepped onto Biola's campus in the fall of 2007, my eyes
were bright with expectation. I remember silently giving up a
prayer of thanksgiving to God for leading me there. My head
swam with expectations. I couldn't wait to encounter God in
ways I never had: I was ready to experience knowledge and fel-
lowship in a new way.

As the weeks passed and the pedestals fell, I began to realize
something was missing: God. I couldn't seem to find Him any-
where and, worse yet, I had almost given up the search. I saw traces
of Him everywhere—in chapel, in classes, even in the Bible verses
taped to the bathroom walls. The problem was, I couldn't *feel*
Him. Having gone to public school all my life, I had always clung
to the verses in Matthew that tell us to be the salt and the light of
the earth. With nonbelievers all around me, the differences in my
beliefs shone like a neon light. But being at a Christian college
was a test of my faith; I didn't know how to let my light be seen
when everyone else's light was shining just as brightly.

I began to accept the distance in my relationship with the
Lord. I relied on chapels and Bible classes for my "fill" of God.

I stopped trying to be an example, since no one around me seemed to need one. But one morning, as I was standing in chapel singing, I realized how many voices could be heard. And that's when it hit me: God doesn't have a statute of limitations. He doesn't tell us to lead a Christlike life *only* if there are people watching. He doesn't tell us to be a light shining on a hill *only* if there are no other lights around. He wants us to live for Him every day, with no exceptions.

So, now as I sit in chapel, listen in class or read the Bible verses taped on the wall, I smile because although I may not be the only light on the hill, I can certainly live a life that adds to the brightness.

Journal Response

Do not conform any longer to the pattern of this world, but be transformed by the renewing of your mind. Then you will be able to test and approve what God's will is—his good, pleasing and perfect will.

ROMANS 12:2

Whether we attend a secular university or a Bible college, we all spend our lives in two different worlds. In what ways do you behave differently in each of those worlds? Are those differences in your life biblical? Are they healthy?

_____
_____
_____
_____
_____
_____
_____

56

Nails

By Kasey Dee Dobbs, Abilene Christian University

Do not let anyone look down on you because you are young, but set an example for the believers in speech, in life, in love, in faith, and in purity.
1 TIMOTHY 4:12

No amount of scraping or scrubbing would budge the dirt and stains under my fingernails. Actually, I knew more than just dirt was under them after gutting a half-century-old bathroom at the summer camp where I was working. The grime I attacked doubtlessly included a heavy amount of rat, bat and raccoon waste, which I had scooped out and swept up as it fell from the ceiling and walls. The war was lost: my nails, which had taken months to grow, had to be cut to rid them of their nastiness.

The awkward feeling of freshly cut, very short fingernails still plagued me as I joined my fellow workers—28 in all—in the dinner line. In front of me was Jessica, a seven-year-old who I reached over to grab a plate.

Jessica bounced her plate impatiently on her forehead. She had also been involved in the "bathroom project," and her fingernails bore evidence similar to mine.

"Woo-ooo!" I said tapping her hand. "You need to cut and clean those nails, girl!"

"Yeah. But I hate that feeling after I cut them." She shook her right hand out in front of her and squished up her face. "It feels yucky."

"I know what you mean." I held out my hands and showed her my nails. "I like to keep mine longer too. But when I can't keep them clean, I cut them to keep all the dirt out. And this week is going to be a dirty one!"

"Yeah." With filthy nails she reached into a bag for a hamburger bun. I wondered why I had bothered to say anything. Why should I think this child would take my advice?

Several days later, I retreated from the work on the bathroom to the solitude of the camp's kitchen where Jessica's mom, Jennifer, was preparing supper. We chatted for several minutes, and then she exclaimed, "Kasey! I owe you big time!"

She almost scared me. "Oh yeah?"

"I overheard you telling Jessica the other day about her nails and how dirty they were." She shook her head. "I'd been trying to cut those nasty things forever! And that night, after you talked to her, she said, 'I think I want my nails short like Kasey's.'"

Recently, I was thinking about the filth in my life and how hesitant I am to get rid of it. Sometimes I am comfortable with the gunk that's built up—my sins, my bad habits, my hang-ups—and don't want to change. I hope as I continue allowing God to cut out and scrub all the sin in my life, I may be an example of a life of purity.

Rags

> *But we are all like an unclean thing, and all our*
> *righteousnesses are like filthy rags.*
> ISAIAH 64:6, *NKJV*

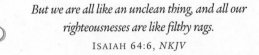

Our own sin can be obvious, but it can also be very hard to detect. There's a certain kind of sin that is especially hard for us to see because we tend to think that God approves of it. Did you ever wonder why Jesus hung out with sinners but reserved His most angry condemnation for those around Him who were the most religious?

It's easy to notice and confess our obvious sins—the lies we tell, the unkind words we say, the things we lust after—but what about our sins of spiritual pride? What about our sins of self-righteousness? Ever feel spiritually smug because you attend church regularly and get called on to teach Sunday School? Ever feel superior because you're the first one ready with a Bible verse for every occasion? It's easy to miss those sins that we mistakenly think God approves of.

But, yeah, our own righteousness is like filthy rags—as dark and dirty as all those other sins we're so aware of and so ready to confess.

57

Stressed to Impress

By Abraham Sherman, Biola University

*Seek the kingdom of God above all else, and live righteously,
and he will give you everything you need.*
MATTHEW 6:33, *NLT*

I should have known I was in for a rough time last semester
when I picked up my 15 textbooks. They were short—only about
300 pages each—but there were 15 of them! Around 5,000 pages
total! All to be read, analyzed and responded to in four months.

I kept up the busy reading schedule for two months, and
then it happened: *burn out*. I finally met my match in workload,
and I was soundly defeated. I engaged in pure damage control
from October to December, scrambling to turn in what I could
when I could. When the dust cleared, I received the worst grades
of my life.

How did I respond to the unrealistic demands of my course-
work? Not too well. I didn't curl up in a fetal position in the corner and cry myself to sleep, but I came close. Only *four* classes.
Sure, they were intensive—but who can't handle four classes?
Was it my academic pride that got me into the situation? Most
likely. Did I pray and thank God for the opportunity to be humbled? I probably should have.

The subjects I was studying were supposedly my forte. I loved
them, but the academic demands overwhelmed me. I loved the

books, but there were too many for me to read. I loved the writing, until the demand for quantity out-shouted quality. I had been a strictly *A* student for eight years straight. Yet last semester, I received three *B*s and a *C*. I'd never gotten that deep into the alphabet before.

I had a scholarly reputation to keep up with family, friends and professors. Further, I had to maintain a high GPA to protect my academic scholarship. Panic hit occasionally. Yet under the weight of my unavoidable responsibilities, I found myself in a place where God could teach me something new.

My fretting didn't help. My pride tried to convince me that maintaining my academic reputation and intellectual self-image were worth enduring unhealthy sleepless nights, skipping chapel and church services and living in distress. Through my seeming failure, God taught me that being perfect was not as important as faithful perseverance. By falling short, I gained a more refined perspective. Rather than continuing to strive to do my academic best, I now had to examine my motives and seek God first.

Here's what my taxing semester taught me: Don't stress to impress. There is only one Person we should seek to make an impression on. God's first concern is not our grades or our reputation for achievement. Maintaining a humble, dependent heart and proceeding with diligence will please Him most.

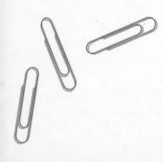

Journal Response

Pride goes before destruction, a haughty spirit before a fall.
Better to be lowly in spirit and among the oppressed than to
share plunder with the proud.

PROVERBS 16:18-19

God has given all of us gifts and talents, and it's easy to focus on those abilities and become proud because of them. What in your life is a source of pride? How might that thing, or things, be a gift better used to advance God's kingdom than your own self-worth?

_____

_____

_____

_____

_____

_____

_____

_____

_____

_____

_____

_____

_____

_____

_____

_____

_____

_____

Living with the Parents

By Andrew M. Obenchain, Boise State University

Honor your father and mother, so that you may live long
in the land the LORD your God is giving you.
EXODUS 20:12

I decided to attend the local university in the town where I grew up. In doing so, there was no need to live in the dorms. Instead, I stayed at home with my parents. I was becoming more independent, making my own schedule with school and getting a part-time job. My parents, realizing how busy I was, gave me fewer responsibilities around the house. I could come and go as I pleased. However, they did have one rule for me: I had a curfew.

At first, the curfew wasn't a big deal. But while I was attending the university, I became active in a few campus organizations and made a lot of friends. Many of those friends lived on campus, which allowed me to experience some of what dorm life had to offer. One thing about living in the dorms appealed to me most: no set curfew. This meant the freedom to do something whenever, without having to worry about the time.

By my second semester, all I wanted to do was hang out with my new friends. I would put homework aside—even skipping a class on occasion—to hang out or have lunch with a friend. I let the social side of college get the best of me. Some of my friends thought it was kind of strange that I sometimes had to rush home to meet my parents' curfew. "You're in college now," they would tell me. "Why should it matter?" I gradually became angry with my parents. "None of my friends have a curfew!" I complained to them.

As a result of hanging out all the time, my grades slipped below average. My parents pointed out that I wasn't fulfilling my calling as a student according to what God commands: "So whether you eat or drink or whatever you do, do it all to the glory of God" (1 Corinthians 10:31). I realized, then, how much I needed to be a better steward of my time, especially as a student.

Do your parents seem unfair at times? We tend to think differently from our parents, especially as we get older and become our own person, but remember that God has given you parents for a reason. Their rules, restrictions and counsel, instead of holding us back, can be the very things that prepare us for the real world ahead.

> *Listen, my son, to your father's instruction and do not*
> *forsake your mother's teaching.*
> PROVERBS 1:8

Meet the Parents

In 1937, *Reader's Digest* attributed the following quote to American humorist and novelist Mark Twain: "When I was a boy of fourteen, my father was so ignorant I could hardly stand to have the old man around. But when I got to be twenty-one, I was astonished at how much the old man had learned in seven years."

One of the great pleasures of becoming an adult is the way it transforms and redefines your relationship with your parents.

They're still your mom and dad—and they always will be. They will still serve godly roles in your life, but both they and you begin to understand each other better. They're no longer controlling monsters, and you're no longer an ungrateful brat.

There will be times of sitting together around a table and straightening out family history. *Yeah, actually I broke that window. No, the hamster didn't really run away.* And there will be rich times of sharing secret worries, smoothing over old grudges, and finally admitting to mistakes.

Enjoy it.

Killing the Weeds

By Jennifer Francois, Liberty University

And now, dear brothers and sisters, one final thing. Fix your thoughts on what is true, and honorable, and right, and pure, and lovely, and admirable. Think about things that are excellent and worthy of praise.

PHILIPPIANS 4:8, *NLT*

When I got to college, I found myself sinking into an abyss of negative thoughts. They started with my dilemma about choosing a major. I began to think something was wrong with me—I wasn't smart enough, I couldn't amount to anything good, and so on and so on. With one thought after another, I bashed myself with negativity. After a while, it didn't take much to depress me, and I didn't feel like "me" anymore.

The next semester, I returned to school and found myself in marching band. Our spiritual theme was "It's All About the Fruit." I'll always remember the devotional that Dr. Elmer Towns, the Dean of our School of Religion, gave one night after a late field practice. He talked on Matthew 13 and told us how to plant our seeds so they had the greatest chance of producing fruit. He told us we had to watch out for the weeds that would spring up among the good seeds and that we'd have to take our gallon—or for some of us even a five- or ten-gallon—jug of weed killer to spray the weeds and allow the fruit to grow.

I immediately thought of all the negative thoughts I had. They were weeds sprung up by Satan. I had allowed the weeds to grow and overtake my good thoughts. From then on, I silently yelled "weed killer!" every time a negative thought entered my mind, stopping it dead in its tracks. I simply refused to let the thought grow any further.

Since then, I've learned how important it is to keep the weeds away daily with "weed killer" and allow God to grow the seeds He has planted in me by staying close to Him through His Word.

Journal Response

Above all else, guard your heart, for it is the wellspring of life.
PROVERBS 4:23

It can be easy—even sometimes fun—to fall into a cynical, pessimistic frame of mind. But is it healthy or productive to stay there? What things are you most cynical about? Is there a healthier or more productive way of thinking about or talking about the same things?

Priesthood, Marriage and Salsa Dancing

By Ricardo Nelson Pineda, Jr., University of Notre Dame

Praise Him with timbrel and dancing.
PSALM 150:4, *NASB*

Ever since my sophomore year of high school, I felt called to be a priest. Many who feel a slight pull to the priesthood are afraid to know if this is their true vocation, because this knowledge might require some great change. I thought I was free from this fear, until my sophomore year of college.

I had a friend with whom I'd go salsa dancing. As I spent more time with her, I became afraid to know if I was called to be a priest. *God has not made it certain*, I told myself. *You could be called to marriage instead.*

What caused me anxiety was the thought of having to give up dancing with my friend because of my newfound affection for her. If I was called to the priesthood, it seemed like playing with fire to dance with someone for whom I had feelings.

Taking the advice of family, I asked myself what would make me happiest: marriage or the priesthood? I imagined that God had prepared a wife who was perfect for me, with whom I would have a great marriage, and that ultimately we'd both make it to heaven. I didn't put a face on her; I just imagined a great marriage. Did I want to pursue that relationship or be a priest? I then thought about all the reasons that I wanted to be a priest. I loved talking about God and His love. I wanted to offer all my love to God and serve Him by helping people come closer to Him. I also remembered my desire to administer the sacraments, especially Eucharist and Penance. Both marriage and the priesthood were good paths, but either one would involve the sacrifice of the other.

In the end, I realized I still wanted to devote my entire life to God as a priest. I came out with a favorable outlook on marriage, even though I came to the conclusion it was not for me. I accepted once again God's call for me to pursue the priesthood, and I felt peace. I would no longer hope for a relationship with my friend.

Since then, I have gone dancing many times and danced with many different girls, including the friend I'd been attracted to. I no longer worry about doubting my call to the priesthood. I'll ask a girl to dance for a song or two, and when it's over, I'll thank her for the dance. I don't know exactly if or when I will be able to dance as a priest. But for now, I think of the line from the movie *My Best Friend's Wedding*: "Maybe there won't be marriage . . . but by God, there'll be dancing."

Call Waiting

We Christians talk a lot about being called, and that's a biblical idea, but what does it really mean? Can we be called to do something we have no interest in doing—like Moses was? Or is "calling" just another word for having a passion for doing something in God's kingdom?

Whatever the term means, how often do we pass up opportunities to try out new ministry opportunities or chances to volunteer because we're not sure if that's where God ultimately
wants us to spend our lives? How often do we let some chance
pass us by because we're not sure we're officially called to it?

If we are offered opportunities to advance God's kingdom,
and they seem like a good fit for our interests and abilities, why
not just assume that God has brought them our way and try
them out? The worst that can happen is that we find out that's
not really our calling after all.

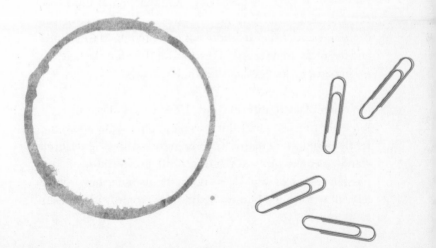

About the Student Authors

Nathan Barstad (Biola University)
Nathan recently graduated from Biola with a degree in design. He enjoys a good movie, conversations with friends and quiet walks where he can do some thinking. One day he hopes to pursue social work so he can help others as he has been helped.

Christine Baumgartner (Biola University)
Christine is an intercultural studies major who will read anything that will stay still long enough. She also loves movies, rain, Disneyland and dolphins. After college, she hopes to acquire a job that will allow her to hang out with kids. Christine hopes to one day learn to fly.

Katy Beers (Biola University)
Katy Beers is studying psychology and theology at Biola University in Southern California. Katy was born and raised in Chicago, and since being at school has come to miss the openness and feel of the Midwest. She is excited for the plans the Lord has for her life and knows that she is in His hands.

Jonathan Blake (California State University, Fullerton)
Jon Blake finished a bachelor's degree in philosophy and is currently working on a master's degree in counseling. He performs stand-up comedy to pass the time until he can realize his true passion—proofreading! He is known for his "refreshingly intellectual" writing and humor. He hopes his comedy is therapeutic as well.

Heather Buchanan (Chapman University)
Heather is a creative writing major at Chapman. She has a brief message for her high school English teacher: *See, Ms. McClure? Somebody likes my writing.*

Bret Burchard (Taylor University)
Bret plays college basketball in the heart of basketball country—Indiana. He believes that God speaks through the things that are important to us and that His truth is proclaimed throughout creation. He encourages others to seek those truths and share them with the world while never forgetting the foundation of faith: love.

Jennifer Campbell (Azusa Pacific University)
Jennifer is studying literature and creative writing, attending every theater performance she can and having pancake parties at midnight (Mickey Mouse pancakes are the best). Because she grew up going to Sunday School, she appreciates Bible classes at APU that enhance her understanding of God's promises.

Adrienne Chaudoin (Taylor University)
Adrienne is a media communications major with a writing concentration. She likes reading in her hammock in the summer and drinking Chai lattes over conversation in the winter. She's always up for a Mario Kart challenge, and her dream job is to write children's books while traveling the world.

Nicole Chin (Azusa Pacific University)
Nicole recently graduated with a bachelor's degree in journalism. As she embarks on her journey into the "real world," Nicole hopes to pursue a career in magazines, either as an editor or a

designer. She is devoted to her friends and encourages them to overcome difficulties.

Pierre Collins (Liberty University)

Pierre is pursuing a bachelor's degree in physical education. He wants to teach and coach football. He is always working to better his life in different areas. His prayer is that God continuously molds him into the man he ought to be.

Becky Compton (Azusa Pacific University)

Becky is pursuing a bachelor's degree in English and a minor in psychology. She plans to teach high school students. Becky has always lived in Southern California and has a short commute. She hopes that through her experiences, she can help others.

Rebekah Cooper (Biola University)

Rebekah is from Fresno, California, and is loving living in Southern California next to Disneyland and the beach. She is currently a communications major with an emphasis in speech and drama and is trying to live a Christlike example every day.

Andrew Lawson Crist (Abilene Christian University)

Andrew prays he will graduate with an English degree from a four-year university without attending school for more than six years to accomplish his goal. At age 22, he is better at dreaming than writing but desires growth and seeks a collaboration of both dreams and skill as he aspires to be a professional writer.

Kasey Dee Dobbs (Abilene Christian University)

Kasey is a true Texan who grew up on a ranch in the Hill Country. She enjoys playing basketball, and she also has a passion for adolescent girls' ministry. Kasey is an English major and plans to write Christian children's books.

Katie Dudgeon (Talbot School of Theology)

Katie graduated from the University of Wisconsin, Madison, with a degree in international relations, and she loves any adventure that involves an airplane. She is passionate about people, personal growth and God. These passions have led her to pursue a master of divinity degree from Talbot School of Theology.

Nathan Fisher (Union University)

Nathan is an English major, hoping to one day teach middle or high school students (possibly at his alma mater). He is a fan of writers Matheson and Poe but enjoys a good rock concert as well. His hope is to help others through teaching and writing alike.

Jennifer Francois (Liberty University)

Jennifer is a Virginia native but loves the Northeast as well as the Tropic South. She is considering majoring in English along with graphic design, or perhaps she'll pursue nursing. She has recently discovered a passion for fiction writing and sharing Bible truths through her stories. She hopes to glorify God through her writing.

Christopher Louis Frank (Miami University)

Chris recently graduated from Miami of Ohio with a degree in business economics. Chris plans to move to Austin, Texas, where he hopes to buy a Vespa, work in a coffee shop, become a movie producer and one day give $250 million to ministry.

Brent Godwin (Auburn University)

Brent is a journalism major at Auburn, where he is involved with Campus Crusade and his local church. He serves as a student recruiter for the University. He loves playing the guitar, singing, and leading worship at weekly meetings. Brent desires to reach people for Christ and to pursue a life of ministry wherever God calls him.

Lauren E. Gossett (Point Loma Nazarene University)
Lauren is pursuing a bachelor's degree in literature with a concentration in English education. She hopes to team up with her father one day to write down the bedtime stories he told to her siblings and her. It is her prayer that her life reflects God's love.

Cathy Hansen (Azusa Pacific University)
Cathy is studying English in Southern California. She is rejoicing in God's faithfulness.

Jamalin Harp (Abilene Christian University)
Jamalin is working toward a degree in English and history. Her career goals are undetermined presently, but she hopes to put her two fascinating majors to good use. She is a San Antonio native and loves Mexican food, travel and spending time outdoors.

Erin Harris (Biola University)
Erin, a born-and-raised San Diego country girl, goes to school in Los Angeles. She is adapting to life in the big city, so she finds great pleasure in turning up Garth Brooks' music to recall the feeling of the country. Erin is an English major who hopes to put her imagination on paper as a professional.

Allison Jean Hart (Santa Clara University)
Allison is from Colorado but attends school in California. She is developing her faith and remembering that "everything happens for a reason."

Laurie K. Hekman (Cornerstone University)

Laurie is an 2008 graduate with a degree in English writing. While in college, Laurie studied abroad at Oxford University, was the editor of her school newspaper, and traveled to South Africa for missions work. Laurie is currently a full-time reporter for *Advance Newspapers* in Jenison, Michigan.

Michelle Hopf (Auburn University)

Michelle Hopf is currently pursuing a degree in English and language arts education. She hopes to teach middle school. She wants to someday open new worlds to others the way countless others have done for her—through writing. Michelle thinks Auburn is the loveliest village on the Plains.

Kristyn Marie Johnson (Corban College)

Kristyn traveled to the Pacific Northwest to study. She is learning to fail in order to succeed.

Alexandra Kerr (Azusa Pacific University)

Alexandra is currently pursuing a bachelor's degree in journalism. A Southern California native, Alexandra plans to study abroad, using her love of writing to examine and explore cultures around the world. It is her wish to experience the beauty of the Lord's creation, seeing the world while spreading His Word.

Kelline Linton (Abilene Christian University)

Kelline is studying in the great state of Texas. She's working on her courage as she follows God.

Lisa Louie (Azusa Pacific University)

Lisa is studying English at a Christian university in Southern California. Originally from Oregon, she is enjoying the sunshine and great Mexican food. She also pole-vaults on the track team and plays alto saxophone in the jazz band. Someday she wishes to teach high school students, helping them discover the freedom that reading and writing literature provides.

Renae Matz (Union University)

Renae, a future world traveler but current resident in West Tennessee, is seeking a degree in English with an emphasis in creative writing, a minor in biblical languages and a possible minor in public relations. She thanks God for the gift of another day.

Mandy McCullough (Belhaven College)

Mandy is a 19-year-old sophomore. She is majoring in creative writing with a music minor. At 14, she felt a call from God to pursue a missions ministry and has already journeyed to Africa. Mandy is active in the college ministry at Country Woods Baptist Church in Byram, Mississippi.

Jessica Mollo (University of Southern California)

Jessica, who is currently studying writing for screen and television, lives to write. She enjoys salsa dance classes and "kickin' it" in Oregon with her sister and nieces. She thanks her mom for her undying support and her late father for instilling in her a wacky sense of humor.

Karla Florence Noles
(New Orleans Baptist Theological Seminary)

After completing her degrees in English and Spanish, Karla moved to New Orleans one year after Hurricane Katrina to attend seminary. She loves working with internationals and hopes one day to combine that love with her passion for writing. Living a life in obedience to God has been the most thrilling yet the most difficult commitment of her life. But she wouldn't trade her journey for the world.

Andrew M. Obenchain (Boise State University)

Andrew is pursuing a bachelor's degree in English with a linguistics emphasis. He's not exactly sure what he wants to do at graduation, but one thing is certain: he wants to glorify God in whatever he pursues and is excited to see God working in his life.

Ricardo Nelson Pineda, Jr. (University of Notre Dame)

Ricardo is graduating from Notre Dame after three years with a philosophy major and theology minor. He plans to pursue his heart's desire of becoming a priest. He has been invited to join the Fathers of Mercy, a Roman Catholic Congregation of Priests based in Kentucky.

Rebecca Whitten Poe (Union University)

Rebecca is a senior at Union University in Jackson, Tennessee. Though she is an English literature major and has worked as an editor, her heart is in her biblical languages minor. She hopes the coming years will find her at seminary pursuing the ministry to which she feels called.

Joshua Prichard (San Francisco State University)

Josh was born in Cincinnati, Ohio, but moved to Southern California when he was young. After escaping, he moved to San Francisco to study cinema at San Francisco State University. The humbly self-proclaimed movie genius says he will regretfully leave the Bay Area one day to join Hollywood's great underworld. Until then . . .

Rebeckah M. Reader (Butler University)

Rebeckah is pursuing a bachelor's degree in media arts and journalism. She has no idea what to do with her life. Until God reveals His plan for her, she will continue to spend her time pondering the mysteries of life and dancing to her iTunes.

Jennifer K. Rickabaugh (Biola University)

Jennifer recently earned a bachelor's degree in liberal studies, with an emphasis in elementary education. She grew up in the Santa Cruz Mountains of California. Jennifer loves the beach and a good cup of coffee. Her prayer is to live a life of pure joy.

Kristen Lynn Sadler (Biola University)

Kristen is an art minor and a psychology major. She loves being with her family in San Diego, running on the beach with her dad, baking with her mom and sharing crazy jokes with her sister. She also enjoys playing her guitar and worshiping God.

Annaruth Sarcone (Kean University)

Annaruth is halfway through a bachelor's degree in speech therapy. She lives in Staten Island and loves the water. In her free time, she loves to jump in puddles, ride horses and read, and she hopes to one day write a novel. Her Savior and her family mean the world to her. She owes them everything.

Lauri Schakett (University of California at Santa Barbara)

Lauri just completed her victory lap (her 5th year) and earned a degree in psychology. As a four-year multi-event athlete for the track team, she successfully aged herself an additional 20 years. Now her ankles crack when she walks around and her knees get stiff when sitting. However, she hopes to be functional long enough to open a holistic center to equip people to live abundant lives.

Dustin Everett Schamaun (Liberty University)

Dustin is currently finishing his degree in philosophy and religion at Liberty University. He feels thankful and always smiles when he realizes that God has woven Himself into the tapestry of all things.

Jessica Schwarzberg (Biola University)

Jessica is majoring in English with a minor in secondary education. She has always enjoyed English and is looking forward to teaching it in the classroom. Her hope is to someday have a library, floor to ceiling, like the one featured in her favorite childhood movie *Beauty and the Beast*.

Abraham Sherman (Biola University)

Prone to wander across Mars and Middle Earth, film major Abraham Sherman returns to reality every now and then to write contemporary screenplays and dabble in theological commentary. He is considering grad school at Talbot Theological Seminary. His first cell phone was purchased in December 2007, under duress.

Junghoo Song (Union University)

Junghoo is pursuing a bachelor's degree in journalism with a minor in English. Having lived in three different countries, he has developed a love for travel and new experiences. He hopes to use his passions to spread God's message through writing and missions.

Elise Toedt (Bethel University)

Elise attends college in Minnesota. She is an education major and wants to serve others.

Jennifer Tibbett (Azusa Pacific University)

A recent recipient of a bachelor's degree in English and writing, Jennifer is currently trying to fathom life post-college. She will soon be deployed for a two-year stint with the Peace Corps and hopes to one day make a career out of music journalism. She thanks God, her wonderful family and beautiful friends for her blessed existence.

Lisa Van Groningen (Trinity Christian College)

Lisa is a recent graduate with a double major in business communication and history. Having gone to school in Chicago for four years, she's learned two very important facts: Chicago is home to amazing food, and one must constantly be trusting God in every aspect of life.

Courtney Jo Veasey
(New Orleans Baptist Theological Seminary)

Courtney is pursuing a master of divinity degree with a concentration in biblical languages. For this broadcast journalism major and former college athlete, seminary has been a challenging yet rewarding lifestyle switch for her. Her greatest claim to fame is being a contestant on *The Price Is Right* game show in 2005.

Christina Waken (California State University, Long Beach)

Christina is an English major with a minor in human resource management. A California girl through and through, she could not be happier than when she is singing and laughing on the beach with her sister. She views life as a great adventure and is passionate about serving the Lord all over the world.

Rachel Watson (Cornerstone University)

Rachel is pursuing a bachelor's degree in journalism. She is also a summer intern at the Grand Rapids Press. In her spare time she writes in what is now volume 24 of the journal she began in seventh grade. She loves stories and hopes to be a feature news reporter who will tell people's untold tales with grace and truth to a world unused to hearing beauty come from the news media.

Kimberly Wilcox (Azusa Pacific University)

Kimberly is pursuing a bachelor's degree in journalism with a minor in English. She enjoys writing for her school newspaper, *The Clause*, and hopes to pursue a career in international correspondence. She also hopes to write novels and settle down in the Midwest to raise a family and passionately follow God's path for her life.

Lynette Woo (Biola University)

Lynette is studying English. She regrets that she will never accomplish her life's dream of being 5′ 3″, so she takes out her frustration by obsessively-compulsively editing her work. When she's not reading, Lynnette watches Asian dramas and drinks boba tea. She also has an unreasonable fear of snails.

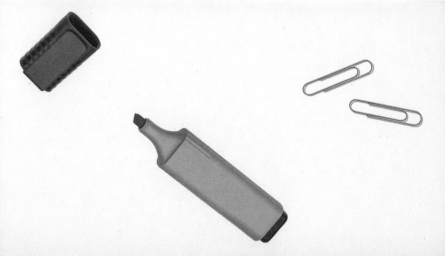

Acknowledgments

Many thanks to our fellow professors who encouraged students to write their stories, especially Alan Blanchard and Cynthia Beach (Cornerstone), Kathy Bruner (Taylor), W. K. Hammersmith (Liberty), Dr. Hawley (NOBTS), Al Haley III and Cole Bennett (ACU), Adrien Lowery, Joseph Bentz, and Marcia Berry (APU). We also appreciate the contributions of Brian Benson, Emily Brown and Michelle Williams, as well as the support of our spouses Gary and Revy, who love us no matter what. Of course, a special note of thanks must go to all of the student contributors who took time to share their experiences.